Rwanda's Gamble

Rwanda's Gamble

✦

Gacaca and a New Model Of Transitional Justice

Peter E. Harrell

Writers Club Press

New York Lincoln Shanghai

Rwanda's Gamble
Gacaca and a New Model Of Transitional Justice

Writers Club Press
an imprint of iUniverse, Inc.

For information address:
iUniverse, Inc.
2021 Pine Lake Road, Suite 100
Lincoln, NE 68512
www.iuniverse.com

ISBN: 0-595-27052-2

Printed in the United States of America

Contents

ACKNOWLEDGEMENTS

First and foremost, I would like to thank Mr. and Mrs. Mike Rugema and their son Moses for their invaluable hospitality and kindness. I could not possible have accomplished what I did in my limited time in Kigali without their assistance.

I would also like to thank everyone who granted my many requests for interviews. I am particularly grateful for the contributions of Kassim Kayira, Gerard Gahima, Chantal van Cutsem, and Klaas De Jonge.

I need to acknowledge Jeffrey Wolf for his willingness to listen patiently to my incessant outpouring of thoughts on the themes of this thesis. To the two of you who read this over and provided commentary—my everlasting thanks. This thesis is immeasurably stronger for your advice.

I should also acknowledge the contribution of the many kind employees at Frist's café, whose coffee substituted for sleep these last few days.

Last but far from least, a particular thank you to Meryl Raymar for your support and words of encouragement that dispelled my too-frequent doubts.

INTRODUCTION

o o o o o o o o o o o o o o o o o o o o o o o o o o o o o o o o o
just
to be able
to bury your body,
to have a place
where your mother
can go with
flowers

—*Ariel Dorfman*

Kibuye town's Catholic church stands on an idyllic hill a half mile or so northeast of the central square. The site affords spectacular views out to Lake Kivu in the west and of the fertile, misty, and banana-tree covered central highlands to the east. The town itself is a provincial resort, quaint in its own way, and Rwandans speak of the area's natural beauty.

Kibuye's tranquility is blissful respite from the merchants and beggars who swarm around any foreigner walking Kigali's streets, and its location a mere two-hour drive from the capital makes it a popular destination for non-governmental organization (NGO) employees, researchers, and Rwandan professionals alike.

Rwanda's roads are reputed to be the best in East Africa, a byproduct of European Union guilt over its inaction during the genocide. Even the most ramshackle of vehicles takes treacherous mountain curves with a nonchalance that raises hairs on the necks of westerners accustomed to designated lanes and speed limits. The views along the road between Kigali and Kibuye would startle someone whose image of

1

Rwanda is dominated by destroyed buildings, machetes, and human remains. People, over half of them children, purposefully walk or bicycle along both sides of the road, carrying on with their business. Merchants hawk their wares in front of any significant cluster of buildings, calling out prices and rejecting bids in the country's universal Kinyarwanda. Brilliantly patterned traditional dresses compete for dominance with clothing cast off from the American heartland. I had to smile at the sight of a t-shirt touting an American school board election in a language its wearer almost certainly did not understand.

Like much of the developing world, Rwanda is a contrast of old and new. People live in mud-and-banana-leaf buildings a stone's throw from signs hawking South African-based cellular carrier MTN's local service, and a call from New York to a cell phone in Kibuye gets through nearly as clearly as it would to a phone a few blocks away.

The Catholic church in Kibuye was my last stop before catching the final scheduled *taxi-minibus* back to Kigali. By the time I arrived, my energy had been sapped by hours spent under the equatorial sun. The air inside the church was cool, a reminder that almost all of Rwanda rises above 5,000 feet and that snow occasionally falls on the volcanic mountains to the north. The church looked as though a clergyman had just finished preparing it for the afternoon service. Someone had swept the floor, arranged the pews, and tended the blooming flowers that graced the altar. Light flooded in through several large stained-glass windows, though the afternoon's lengthening shadows kept me checking my watch. I was the only visitor, and though my guidebook had mentioned something about a guide, he was not in evidence. I looked into the confessional booth, took a few photographs, and admired the bit of religious art hung on one of the walls. Mostly I sat, reflected, and appreciated the almost unnatural calm that was a welcome contrast to the ubiquitous East African greeting of foreigners—"Mzungu! Mzungu!"—and the incessant questions of those who spoke a bit of French.

My guidebook had listed this particular church as a genocide memorial, a fact confirmed by a large sign along the main road. But unlike memorials that play on the shock value of stacked bones or, in one case, several thousand human skulls, this particular church derives its eloquence from its very silence. Only as I left did I notice a small glass case of human remains that served to commemorate the lives taken.

In April of 1994, a journalist would have borne witness to a very different scene. Rwanda was on edge following the murder of Burundian leader Melchior Ndadaye at the hands of Tutsi military officers. President Habyarimana's propagandists were fanning ethnic tensions by broadcasting exaggerated rumors of Tutsi attacks in the north. On the evening of April 6th, still-unidentified assailants drove up the hill overlooking Kigali's airport and used a light anti-aircraft missile to destroy Habyarimana's incoming presidential jet.

A tense calm reigned in Kibuye for another few April days even as militias allied with the newly formed extremist government began openly killing Tutsi residing in the capital. Witnesses recount that the violence reached Kibuye on the evening of the 11th or morning of the 12th. By the 13th, large numbers of Tutsi had abandoned their homes and fled. Extremist militias quickly tacked up roadblocks where Tutsi were taken aside to be murdered just out of sight of passersby. Those fortunate enough to escape that immediate fate sought refuge in public buildings, where they had been spared during previous times of violence. Hospitals, schools, stadiums, and churches were soon overrun with Tutsi hoping against hope that no one would be killed in such public spaces. By April 14, the Kibuye town's church was sanctuary to some 4,000 refugees.[1]

Local gendarmes and trucked-in militia members surrounded the church on April 15, but the cornered refugees used rocks and sticks to beat back the initial half-hearted attacks. Stalemate reigned for two days, as those on the inside watched their supplies dwindle and tried to cover their ears against the taunts of their captors, many of them neighbors or colleagues. Then, about 10AM on the morning of April 17, the local prefect Clement Kayishema drove up in a white Toyota and read aloud a statement urging that the militia "get to work," words understood by all to mean massacring the Tutsi.[2] Accounts differ on whether he personally shot off three warning bullets. Regardless, militiamen acting on his orders opened fire on the church and tossed grenades through the shattered windows. Flaming tires were used to soften up any resistance before Kayishema led a force inside to hunt survivors.[3] One witness recounted that Kayishema personally took the life of an infant before departing to lead other groups of killers elsewhere.[4]

Zambian authorities cooperating with international investigators arrested Kayishema in Lusaka on May 2, 1996, ending a comfortable exile that began when he fled Rwanda and took a position with an international NGO working in Zaire.[5] He was transferred to the custody of the United Nation's International Criminal Tribunal for Rwanda (ICTR), and was flown to Arusha later that month. On landing, he became the third and then-most prominent person indicted for crimes stemming from the Rwandan genocide.[6] Three years later, he was convicted on most charges—including the attack in Kibuye—and sentenced to serve four life sentences.[7] Kayishema stands very little chance of ever again seeing the towns he brutalized or, for that matter, anything beyond the gloomy confines of his prison cell.

Since the Allied trials of Nazi leaders at Nuremburg, elements of the international legal community have pressed for the prosecution of men like Clement Kayishema. He is guilty by any standard of crimes against the conscience of humanity, but until the tearing-down of the Berlin Wall, Cold War politics and Great Power alliances prevented any serious international attempts to prosecute state officials. Since 1990, however, there has been a renewed interest in holding state officials accountable for crimes they commit against their own people.

It is perhaps too early to speak of universally accepted guidelines for this "transitional justice," but the outlines of a three-fold model are emerging: an international tribunal to prosecute top-level regime members, national-level prosecution of their subordinates, and a truth commission to document a regime's crimes for posterity. A South African-style truth commission that grants amnesty for truth is offered as a sort of second-best option if political realities preempt prosecution.[1]

I term this the "liberal-prosecutorial model of transitional justice" because it is based on a liberal conception of human rights and retributive notions of justice that require the prosecution of wrongdoers.

The liberal-prosecutorial model of transitional justice holds that criminal accountability for state-sponsored crimes can achieve several important ends.[8] Morally, such prosecutions satisfy the victims' right to justice. From a utilitarian perspective, it is held to (1) reduce nationalism and ethnic tension by assigning individuals, not groups, responsibility for abuses, (2) dissipate calls for vengeance, (3) deter future human rights violations, (4) promote the rule of law, and (5) build support for democracy.[9]

The liberal-prosecutorial model of transitional justice emerged from a relatively small number of democratic transitions in Europe and, to a lesser extent, Latin America. All of these transitions shared certain commonalities: a small number of wrongdoers relative to their victims and to the population as a whole, and reasonably modern economies and social structures

Despite the model's origin in a particular set of circumstances, it is increasingly viewed as universally applicable. The international com-

---

1.   Several political scientists and international lawyers disagree with this characterization of truth commissions as "second best," arguing that their goals differ from those of prosecution and that they can be independently valuable. I think that the emerging model of transitional justice accepts this argument, but believes that the two should work in tandem.

munity's decision to create essentially identical international tribunals for Rwanda, Yugoslavia, and now Sierra Leone—despite significant differences between the three nations' transitional situations—is indicative of the liberal-prosecutorial model's growing clout. International ratification of the Rome Statute of the International Criminal Court would give the model greatly expanded jurisdiction, and could ensure its dominant position in international law for decades to some.

In this thesis, I will argue that the emerging liberal-prosecutorial model of transitional justice is not appropriate in all transitional contexts. A short comparison of two nations where human rights advocates have urged the adoption of liberal-prosecutorial justice, Rwanda and Chile, is illustrative.

Augusto Pinochet's long-running dictatorship was responsible for 3,197 "disappearances" before finally falling from grace in 1990.[10] The governments that have succeeded the General have been liberal and democratic, while natural wealth and the embrace of free-market economics have given Chile a gross national product approaching that of poorer European nations. Chilean survivors in Santiago and elsewhere may occasionally cross paths with the relatively few number of government officials and military who carried out Pinochet's violence, but these incidents are isolated and a far from routine part of daily life.

On the other hand, Rwandans are trying to put their country together after a genocide that took a million lives. As many as 200,000 Rwandans, out of a population of 8 million, directly participated in the slaughter, and hundreds of thousands more may have engaged in opportunistic looting and other property crime. Today, Rwanda remains a desperately poor nation where millions live on less than a dollar a day and 90 percent of the people eke out their livelihoods as subsistence farmers. A predominantly Tutsi undemocratic government continues to rule, although it has begun to democratize villages' governing councils. Most Rwandan survivors live side by side with killers or their families, and share their communities' public resources.

It is absurd to think that one model of justice could be appropriate in both these situations. On one level, Rwanda quite literally cannot afford the sort of courts that Chile could. On another level, however, the two countries need justice to accomplish very different ends. Chile arguably needs justice to consolidate its democratic government, to deter potential coups, and to consolidate the rule of law. Rwanda, I will argue, needs justice for fundamentally different reasons: to eliminate the popular morality that tolerated genocide, to ensure security, and to promote reconciliation.[11] Only recently has either Rwanda or the international community begun to recognize that Rwanda's material realities and these goals will require a fundamentally different model of transitional justice.

The Rwandan Patriotic Front (RPF), the one-time rebel group that now governs the country, is dominated by Rwandan Tutsis who fled the first waves of ethnic violence in the late 1950s and 1960s. Most members spent time in exile in Uganda and Kenya. Many of those at the top honed their military skills fighting in the bush with Yoweri Musoveni while they dreamed of return to their homeland. They, and not the international community, invaded in 1994, defeated the genocidal regime, and declared themselves the national government. Given this history, it was not surprising that the RPF leadership came to power promising to bring the genocidaires[2] to justice.

They initially sought justice using the liberal-prosecutorial model. Their representative to the UN pushed for an international tribunal[3], and by late 1994 RPF forces began taking suspects into custody for trial by domestic courts. The numbers quickly surpassed expectations. Before coming to power, the RPF predicted that it would try 2,000

---

2. In Rwanda, this French word has come to refer to those who participated in the genocide.
3. Ironically, Rwanda was the lone Security Council member to vote against the ICTR. I will address this in the next chapter, but its concerns were primarily with the Tribunal's location in Tanzania, pre-emption of Rwandan courts, and inability to impose the death penalty.

people for genocide,[12] but the actual number of killers may be a hundred times as large—some 120,000 suspects are currently in prison.[13] Ugandan political scientist Mahmood Mamdani recorded one RPF official's reaction in 1994: "When we captured Kigali, we thought we would face criminals in the state. Instead, we faced a criminal population."[14]

From the outset, the genocide's destruction has crippled efforts to bring genocidaires to justice. The International Criminal Tribunal for Rwanda (ICTR), in Arusha, suffered from shortages of investigators and office space, poor communication with the Rwandan government, language barriers, and physical and emotional distance from the site of the crimes it was investigating. The ICTR is prosecuting a veritable "Who's Who" of the genocidal government, but it does not believe that it has a mandate to try anyone except top government officials. This provides scant comfort to Rwandan survivors living in houses along side their attackers.

Rwanda's domestic prosecutions have been similarly hampered. Six years after Rwanda began its prosecutions, 6,000 suspects have been tried. The plight of the 120,000 others languishing in prison is almost Kafkesque. They often do not know what they are accused of, and even more frequently lack access to lawyers. Most tragically, Rwanda's courts will require well over a century to clear their caseload. In a country with an average life expectancy of 49,[15] few prisoners will survive until their court date. Given that state prosecutors themselves estimate 15 percent of those arrested are innocent, this situation is by any standard a miscarriage of justice.[16] Those who killed on Kayishema's orders can probably be seen working on communal projects around Kibuye, dressed in the ridiculous pink pajamas that serve as prison uniforms, awaiting trials they will never see.

Meanwhile, the cost of maintaining these prisons has constrained the government's ability to implement popular and much needed development projects. The generally strong young men in prison are unable to help rebuild a nation badly in need of reconstruction.

Rwanda's poverty requires that the nation balance justice against practical concerns—and the current justice system is not sustainable.

These material realities prompted the government in 1999 to begin searching for a "third way" that would promote criminal accountability without continuing to bankrupt the nation. In mid-2000, it decided to embark on a radical experiment. It drafted a law modernizing "gacaca," an indigenous form of dispute resolution mediated by village elders, and gave 11,000 newly-created "gacacas" jurisdiction to try all but the most heinous crimes. On October 4, 2001, Rwandans elected over a quarter of a million judges to sit on these gacacas. By late 2002, these elected judges will begin collecting evidence and hearing the cases of suspects. The process is expected to last 3 to 5 years.

My thesis will argue that gacaca is a promising step for Rwanda. The liberal-prosecutorial model of transitional justice was simply inappropriate and unworkable in the Rwandan context, and a new model of justice was needed.

I will argue that post-genocide Rwanda—which is characterized by a high level of complicity in atrocity and settlement patterns that intersperse victims and victimizers—is well suited to benefit from what I term the "communitarian restorative model of transitional justice." This model is predicated on restorative as well as retributive principles, and may be able to promote moral reform, security, and reconciliation despite Rwanda's poverty, poor education, and often non-existent communications systems. I then argue that gacaca incorporates numerous elements of this model, and consequently offers Rwanda its best hope for justice and reconciliation.

Chapter 1 examines the history leading up to the genocide. It discusses both proximate causes—the civil war, the polarization of politics, and finally Habyarimana's murder—and the longer-term development of tension between Rwanda's Hutu and Tutsi. Several excellent books, notably Alison Des Forges *Leave None to Tell the Story: Genocide in Rwanda,* have been written on the subject and this chapter will do little more than summarize their findings. However, the historical context of 1994 is a necessary background to any assessment of justice in its aftermath.

Chapter 2 turns to justice. It questions the purpose of pursuing justice in the aftermath of mass atrocity. It argues that justice in societies such as post-genocidal Rwanda serves different ends than justice in other transitional contexts. It then examines how a communitarian restorative model of justice can better address those ends than the prevailing liberal-prosecutorial model.

Chapter 3 describes Rwanda's gacaca jurisdictions, discussing jurisdiction, procedure, and implementation. Chapter 4 analyzes parallels between gacaca and the communitarian restorative model of justice, and argues that as a form of communitarian restorative justice, gacaca is well suited to Rwanda.

The concluding Chapter 5 very briefly recommends policies to ensure gacaca's successful implementation. In closing, I look at the wider need for communitarian restorative justice elsewhere. Gacaca is a promising beginning to a model of justice badly needed across much of Africa.

In many respects, it is too early to assess accurately gacaca's ability to promote security, justice and reconciliation. Judicial training begins this month (April 2002), and the first trials are at least a year away. The critics may yet prove the merits of their argument that gacaca will collapse under the collected weight of judicial bias and violations of defendants' rights. Even if those fears are realized, however, the fact remains that the current system of justice in Rwanda was broken and that the only viable replacement will be based on the communitarian restorative model of transitional justice.

1

HISTORY

"We both, Hutu, Tutsi, came from somewhere else a long
time ago."

—*Tutsi woman*

America's press portrayed the Rwandan genocide as yet another
example of ancient tribal strife destroying a nation. Even our national
newspaper of record, the *New York Times*, wrote on April 12, 1994 of
"the blood lust and ancient ethnic hatreds that have once more
inflamed Rwanda."[17] But this characterization of Rwanda's past—as
even journalists now admit—misrepresents "tribes" that trace their
roots to the late 19th century and ethnic tensions of even more recent
origins.

The first Europeans to enter the Kingdom of Rwanda towards the
end of the 19th century found a country of striking beauty. The open,
game-covered savannah of the east breaks and rises dramatically, with
the misty volcanoes of the north peaking at over 14,000 feet. The
country's innumerable hills are lush shades of green broken by the
dreamy blue of mountain lakes. The land is fertile, and today almost all
of the forest that once covered Africa's Great Rift Valley has given way
to bananas, potatoes, and cattle. These early European visitors saw a
somewhat less garden-like, but already intensely cultivated land.

The people were equally welcoming. German Count von Goetzen,
sent in 1894 to inform the Rwandans that their country had been a

German protectorate since the Congress of Vienna in 1881, received a welcome almost too hospitable for his taste. He later wrote, "Feeling strong and being moderately equipped with weapons, we certainly would have liked to [fight] a more serious enemy."[18]

Von Goetzen found a linguistically, religiously, and culturally homogenous population that was divided into three groups: the Hutu, the Tusti and the much less numerous Twa.[19] The three groups lived side-by-side, spoke the same Bantu language, and occasionally intermarried. Tutsi comprised about 15% of the population and were generally the wealthiest and most powerful of the groups, but their preeminence was by no means exclusive.

Rival *mwami,* sacred kings who physically embodied the essence of their kingdoms, feuded for control over present-day Rwanda.[20] These *mwami* ruled over a complex hierarchy of both *abiiru* (religious officials) and local chiefs with responsibility over men (fighting), land (and taxation), and pastures (cattle grazing).[21] One person could be responsible for all three chiefly functions, but they could also be divided among several rivals.[22]

European colonial administrators would establish indirect rule over Rwanda, a decision that had powerful ramifications for its political life and ethnic identity. Before analyzing colonial views of Rwandan society and the policies that flowed from them, however, we must look at what preceded the Europeans' arrival.

Pre-colonial Rwanda

The origins of the three ethnic groups remain unclear, though the Twa (less than 1 percent of the population at colonization) were almost certainly Rwanda's original inhabitants. Genetic studies dating from the late 1980s suggest that the Hutu and the Tutsi are descended from at least two different waves of immigrants—the Hutu are a legacy of the Bantu expansion across East Africa while Tutsi immigrated later, apparently from a non-malarial region.[23] Similar studies indicate that there has been substantial intermarriage over the years.[24]

The pastoralist Tutsi were probably on average richer than the Hutu, and their *mwamis* disproportionately powerful. However, the Tutsi did not immediately assume a dominant position. Neither group seems to have developed a strong sense of ethnic identity prior to the 19th century.

Catherine Newbury is a researcher at the University of North Carolina who has studied Ijwi Island in Lake Kivu, which has a similar ethnic composition to Rwanda but has not shared its political development. Based on her studies, it appears that clan membership was traditionally the important part of Rwandan identity. On Ijwi, "Tutsi" status derives from some combination of ancestry and wealth, while "Hutu" has no clear meaning[25]—indicating that relatively recent political events gave "Hutu" and "Tutsi" their contemporary significance in Rwanda.[26] Newbury's studies accord with early colonial accounts that wealth was as significant a factor in "ethnic" identity as genealogy. Missionary Father Léon Classe, for example, wrote:

> It should be noted that the term "Tutsi" often refers not to origin but to social condition, or wealth, especially as regards to cattle: whoever is a chief, or who is rich will often be referred to as Tutsi....[27]

Nineteenth-century statebuilding by an ascendant and self-consciously Tutsi Mwami line, the Abanyiginya of Nduga in central Rwanda, was likely the catalyst that transformed loose identities into the rigid ethnic groups one finds today. This line's last and greatest independent king, Mwami Rwabugiri (reign 1860–95), led military campaigns to consolidate most of present-day Rwanda under his rule.[28] Faced with the problems of governing over fractious elites, Rwabugiri dismissed officials from traditionally powerful families and replaced them with men dependent on him; he divided administrative duties to ensure that power was balanced among several individuals; and he appointed his courtiers to rule provinces that had historically retained a degree of independence.[29]

Rwabugiri's successful conquests forced him to develop heuristic devices for choosing administrators to govern the newly conquered territories. One such device used to ensure loyalty was a person's Tutsi status.[30] State development and the growing power of government slowly increased the divide between Rwabugiri's Tutsi administrators and those they governed until two distinct groups emerged. "Hutu," instead of merely connoting "not Tutsi," emerged as a subaltern counter-identity. Newbury writes:

> The statebuilding efforts of Rwabugiri heightened awareness of ethnic differences in Kinyaga [a province she studied]. With the arrival of [court] authorities, lines of distinction were altered and sharpened, as the categories of Hutu and Tuutsi (*sic*) assumed new hierarchical overtones associated with proximity to the central court—proximity to power. Later, when the political arena widened, these classifications became increasingly stratified and rigidified. More than simply conveying the connotation of cultural difference from Tuutsi, Hutu identity came to be associated with and eventually defined by inferior status. [31]

Mamood Mamdani finds supporting causes for this 19th century divergence between the Tutsi and the Hutu in two arenas: religion and the client-patron relationships that characterized pre-colonial economic life.

Since the 16th century, Rwandan kings had been obliged to periodically perform a series of rituals that promoted the national welfare; collectively they were known as *ubiiru*. Supervising the *ubiiru*—and serving as chief advisors to the king in military matters—were three top *abiiru*, at least one of whom was of Hutu lineage. According to Mamdani, "The *abiiru*…were also the institution through which important Hutu lineages were incorporated into the Rwandan state."[32] In the late 18th century the founder of the Abanyiginya line, however, undertook a series of religious reforms that weakened the power of the *abiiru* and freed himself from his ritual prescriptions—simultaneously weakening non-Tutsi authority.

The 19th century also bore witness to changes in the client-patron relationships that structured Rwandan economic behavior. Prior to Rwabugiri's reign, clientship existed primarily as a means for middle-class families to obtain military protection and land rights in exchange for work or goods (cattle), or for families to elevate their social status by entering into agreements with superiors.[33] Rwabugiri witnessed the expansion of two new forms of clientship, *ubuletwa* and *ubuhaki,* which proliferated at the expense of earlier varieties of patron-client relationships. Both of these relationships broke with tradition by binding individuals, not families, to patrons.[34] *ubuhaki,* also reversed the traditional flow of cattle, and had a particularly deleterious impact on lower-class clients. Patrons now provided clients with cattle in exchange for repressive corvée labor and demands of gifts. Not surprisingly, patron demands escalated over time. Under *mwami* Rwabugiri, the effect of these changes was to further expand Tutsi wealth and power at the expense of other groups.[35] Disparate individuals who had previously affiliated with one of numerous clan groupings increasingly coalesced into a Hutu "imagined community" defined by opposition to Tutsi dominance.[36]

The Colonial Era

Colonial notions of Rwandans' origins were grounded more in late-19th century European ideas than in these precolonial Rwandan realities. John Hanning Speke, a British explorer best known for tracing the Nile to Lake Victoria, argued that most of the East and Central African nations he visited consisted of indigenous agriculturalists ruled by superior pastoralist conquerors. In one widely influential book, Speake wrote:

> In these countries [East-central Africa] the government is in the hands of foreigners, who had invaded and taken possession of them, leaving the agricultural aborigines to till the ground, while

junior members of the usurping clans herded cattle—just as in Abyssinia.... [37]

Speake's views both accorded with and influenced the "Hamitic hypothesis" that structured 19th century European views of African political life. According to this hypothesis, ruling African groups were descendants of the Biblical figure Ham—corrupted, but remaining superior to the Nubians, Ethiopians, and other African peoples.[38] In Rwanda (and Burundi), Tutsi power and pastoral wealth at the time of colonization led colonial agents to conclude that they were the natural, Hamitic rulers.[39]

Perceived racial differences reinforced this idea of Tutsi superiority. If colonials saw the Hutu as "short and thick-set with a big head, jovial expression, a wide nose and enormous lips....who like to laugh and lead a simple life,"[40] the Tutsi were something else altogether. One colonial report glowed:

> The [Tutsi] of a good race has nothing of the negro, apart from his color. He is usually very tall, 1.80 m. at least.... He is very thin, a characteristic which tends to be even more noticeable as he gets older. His features are very fine: a high brow, thin nose and fine lips framing beautiful shining teeth.... Gifted with a vivacious intelligence, the Tutsi displays a refinement of feelings which is rare among primitive people. He is a natural-born leader, capable of extreme self-control and of calculated goodwill.[41]

Combined, these views of Tutsi superiority had a profound impact on patterns of colonial rule. This was particularly true after Belgium conquered Rwanda and neighboring Burundi in 1916, marking the beginning of sweeping governmental reforms. Belgium combined the two countries for administrative purposes. Ruling such a large territory in a cost-effective manner required the cooperation of local elites, a fact well recognized by Belgium's first Resident, Pierre Ryckmans:

The co-operation of the kings constitutes an indispensable element of progress and civilization…Without them the problem of government would remain insoluble.[42]

But the cooperation of *mwamis* alone was insufficient to maintaining order; the colonial administration also had to ensure that local chiefs were loyal to their superiors and ultimately the colonial administration. Belgian reforms intended ensure such loyalty had the effect of strengthening Tutsi power and making the division between Hutu and Tutsi even more rigid.

In 1926 Rwanda's colonial Resident Charles Voisin reduced the number of local chiefs and centralized their appointment process. Although the administration originally made an effort to ensure Hutu representation in the reformed government, objections from the Catholic Church and other Tutsi supporters prompted the dismissal of almost all Hutu officials.[43] By 1959 forty-three of forty-five chiefs and 549 of 559 sub-chiefs were Tutsi.[44] Reducing the number of local chiefs further elevated their power by reducing the opportunity for peasants to engage in their traditional practice of playing chiefs off against each other. This resulted in substantially harsher patterns of rule.[45]

A separate series of reforms further altered patron-client interactions. *Ubuletwa* service to local chiefs was made obligatory for all male Hutu,[46] and a new form of labor, *akazi,* was introduced as an annual requirement of several weeks of work on state-sponsored projects.[47] The individual rather than familial nature of the reformed *ubuletwa* and new *akazi* labor curtailed the peasant strategy of "[delegating] a strong young good-for-nothing to sweat for all its members"[48] and meant that demands on peasants escalated even as chiefs' power became more despotic. This further entrenched Hutu as a subaltern oppositional identity.

Education was the third arena of pro-Tutsi bias in colonial policy. Church run schools had begun favoring Tutsi students as early as 1913 to cement a colonial alliance with the ruling class. Discrimination in admissions continued as official policy through the Second World War. Rwanda's principle college, in Butare, took five to ten times as many Tutsi as Hutu. Aside from two theological seminaries at Kabgayi and Nyikibanda, post-secondary education was completely closed to Hutu, and Hutu seminary graduates rarely found fulfilling work.[49]

Church-run schools opened their doors to Hutu in the late 1940s. Discrimination in the workplace, however, continued—spurring the development of an educated but disenchanted Hutu counter-elite.

Colonial policy "hardened" ethnic identity by severely limiting opportunities to switch ethnic groups. Intermarriage, as indicated earlier, was tolerated if not common, and the phenotypical continuity between Hutu and Tutsi had traditionally allowed successful individuals to become "Tutsified." There are even accounts of religious ceremonies formalizing this process.[50]

The colonial administration held the first Rwandan census in 1933–1934, and the subsequent issuing of national identity cards listing ethnicity effectively ended movement between the two major groups. Ironically, Belgian criteria for determining Tutsi status are not quite clear. Some claim that class difference was the determining factor, but others who have compared census data with economic statistics believe that a combination of class and genealogy must have been used.[51]

In this light, Rwanda's supposedly ancient ethnic identities look surprisingly modern in origin. Tutsi gained clear superiority only after 1860, and it was the escalating harshness of their rule that instilled in the governed a "Hutu" ethnic consciousness. After the hardening of the two ethnic groups in the mid 1930s, the Hutu "began to experience the solidarity of the oppressed."[52]

Independence and Its' Aftermath

Rwanda was as captivated as any African nation by the anti-colonial sentiments that quickened hearts across the continent following the Second World War. Rwandan elites, if not Belgian administrators, realized by the late 1940s that the colonial regime was waning. However, the hardened Hutu-Tutsi split—and the emergence of a nascent Hutu counter-elite—injected competing ethnic agendas into the decolonization movement. The Tutsi leadership, sensing that growing calls for democratization would undermine their power, agitated for rapid decolonization to be completed before any Hutu movements consolidated into an effective political force.[53] The Hutu counter-elite, conversely, desired that the colonial regime first democratize Rwanda's indigenous government and then grant the nation independence.

Under United Nations pressure, the colonial administration held elections for "advisory councils" at every level of Rwandan government in 1953. The Tutsi leadership, however, refused to relinquish control over the nominations of candidates. The result was "a process of diffusion of power but principally among the group which already possessed it, that is to say the Tutsi caste."[54] 90.6 percent of those elected to the top *Counseil Supérieur du Pays,* for example, were Tutsi.[55] The next elections, in 1956, were freer, but indirect elections for top officials ensured continued Tutsi dominance. Continued Tutsi control, despite elections, "convinced the Hutu political elite that nothing short of political power would crack the Tutsi hold on social, economic, and cultural resources."[56]

The year 1957 marked a turning point in Rwandan history. A UN decolonization team on a routine visit was greeted by two documents outlining rival visions of the country's future.[57] The *mwami's* High Council presented its *Mise au Point,* which called for rapid decolonization and a transfer of power to the Tutsi *mwami* and his advisors.[58] Grégoire Kayibanda and 8 other Hutu intellectuals presented the other document, *Notes on the Social Aspect of the Racial Native Problem in Rwanda,* more popularly known as the *Bahutu Manifesto.*[59] The *Manifesto* proclaimed the need for a double liberation of Rwanda's Hutu, from both the European colonials and the equally oppressive and foreign "Hamite" Tutsi:[60]

> The problem is above all a problem of political monopoly which is held by one race, the Tutsi; political monopoly which, given the totality of current structures becomes an economic and social monopoly which, given the *de facto* discrimination in education, ends up being a cultural monopoly, to the great despair of the Hutu who see themselves condemned to remain forever subaltern manual labourers and still worse, in the context of an independence which they will have helped to win without knowing what they are doing.[61]

Gregoire Kayibanda had been born near Kabgaya town in 1923; the son, it was said, of a Congolese father and a Hutu mother. He attended the seminary at Nyakibanda and took a job teaching near Kigali after he received his degree. In the early 1950s, a career change brought him home to Kabgaya, where he became the editor of modest newspaper. Following the paper's closure in 1956, Kayibanda became increasingly active in Hutu political causes and, a year later, found himself a leading author of the *Manifesto*[62].

The two rival documents unleashed a torrent of pent-up political emotions. Kayibanda formed Rwanda's first real political party, the Mouvement Sociale Muhutu (MSM), in June of 1957.[63] The MSM was a vehicle to promote the *Manifesto's* ideology, and other individuals with their own political ideas quickly followed Kayibanda's lead. By 1959, four dominant parties vied for the electorate: Kayibanda's reconstituted MSM, now the Mouvement Démocratique Rwandais/Parti du Mouvement et de l'Emancipation Hutu (MDR-PARMEHUTU); Joseph Gitera's Association pour la Promotion Sociale de la Masse, officially multi-ethnic but Hutu-dominated; the conservative Tutsi-dominated Union National Rwandais (UNAR); and the Rassemblement Démocratique Rwandais, the one sincerely multi-ethnic party. [64]

In 1958, elderly members of the *mwami's* court retaliated for the *Manifesto* and other Hutu political demands by issuing a provocative statement that claimed the *mwami's* ancestors had come to power by conquering the Hutu tribes and that "there could be no basis for brotherhood between Hutu and Tutsi."[65] Although this extreme view embarrassed more moderate Tutsi leaders, their growing sense that both domestic politics and the colonial regime were turning against them helped maintain Tutsi unity.[66] 1

The great political scientist Crawford Young writes that "competitive elections...[have the effect] of catalyzing fears and insecurities and mobilizing cultural identities."[67] The campaign leading up to Rwanda's national elections, called for late 1959, certainly polarized the nation along ethnic lines.

The elections began to unravel on July 25, 1959, when Rwanda's *mwami* Mutara passed away under suspicious circumstances; many Tutsi believed the Belgian authorities had poisoned him.[68] The court's conservative faction broke with precedent and appointed a political figurehead at Mutara's funeral on July 28, spurring Hutu suspicions of an extremist Tutsi plot to retain power in the face of an expected Hutu victory at the polls.[69] Kayibanda's MDR-PARME-HUTU and APROSOMA responded by escalating anti-Tutsi ethnic rhetoric, touching off a cycle of accusations and counter-accusations. Francois Rukeba of the pro-monarchy UNAR, for example, insinuated that those demanding democratic reforms were guilty of treason:

> The whole of Africa is struggling against colonialism, the same colonialism which has exploited our country and destroyed our

---

1.   Belgian archival documents indicate that by the early 1950s Tutsi demands for power had begun to turn colonial agents against their traditional allies.[1] The *mwami* himself became aware of these changing sympathies when the Belgian government offered him an uncharacteristically chilly reception in Brussels in 1958, and colonial-Tutsi relations became quite strained on his return. (Lemarchand, *Rwanda and Burundi*. 155)

ancestral customs in order to impose alien ones upon us. The goal
of our party is to restore these customs, to shake off the yoke of
Belgian colonialism, to reconquer Rwanda's independence. To
remake our country we need a single party like UNAR, based upon
tradition and no other ideology. He who does not belong to this
party will be regarded as the people's enemy, the Mwami's enemy,
Rwanda's enemy.[70]

In November, ethnic rhetoric degenerated into violence. UNAR
supporters attacked a Hutu sub-chief and PARMEHUTU member on
the first of the month, provoking a violent Hutu retaliation. Rioters
torched thousands of homes and attacked Tutsi residents of Gitarama,
Ruhengeri, Gisenyi, and Kibuye. Hundreds were killed in the Hutu
attacks and Tutsi retaliations.[71] Tens of thousands of Tutsi fled to
neighboring Tanzania and Uganda, taking up residence in hastily
established UN refugee camps near Rwanda's borders.

Belgium responded to this crisis by dispatching Colonel Bem Guy
Logiest, who arrived on November 4 with nearly absolute powers and a
mandate to restore order. Logiest maintained that Tutsi dominance
was the cause of Rwanda's problems and that the solution was Hutu
empowerment through rapid democratization. Not long into his ten-
ure, he declared, "Because of the force of circumstances, we have to
take sides. We cannot remain neutral and passive."[72] He replaced
hundreds of Tutsi administrators with Hutu, who, though popular,
lacked experience and were ill-prepared for the responsibilities of government.[73]

November's elections were rescheduled to June and July of 1960
despite continuing ethnic tensions and a UNAR boycott. Kayibanda's
PARMEHUTU won an overwhelming victory. It took 2390 of 3125
total Communal Council seats,[74] and Hutu burgomasters were
elected in 210 of Rwanda's 229 communes. After the election, Logiest
declared that, "the [Hutu] revolution is over."[75]

Formal decolonization unfolded almost as an afterthought. Over the night of January 27–28, 1961, thousands of burgomasters convened in the lively provincial city of Gitarama. The meeting's pretense was a discussion of "the maintenance of peace and order," but those in attendance understood the true purpose: late on the afternoon of January 28, the assemblage proclaimed Rwanda a free republic and elected Grégoire Kayibanda its Prime Minister.[76]

Following Belgium's grant of formal independence the next year, President Kayibanda and his PARMEHUTU consolidated their rule at the expense of both Hutu and Tutsi political opponents. The President quickly adopted the distant, authoritarian rule that once characterized Rwanda's *mwami*—prompting one historian to write that Kayibanda "was in fact the *mwami* of the Hutu."[77] He promoted an ideology of Hutu worth, majoritarianism, work, and Christian morality, he stifled politics, and—beyond including a few token Tutsi in his first cabinet—did nothing to restore ethnic harmony.[78]

This unfolding of independence, particularly the dramatic reversal of the Tutsi's fortunes, was to have a lasting impact on Rwanda's history. By 1967, some 20,000 Tutsi had been killed in waves of violence and another 300,000 refugees had fled abroad.[79] Kayibanda's own description of ethic relations at independence would accurately characterize them for the duration of his rule:

> Two nations in a single state…Two nations between whom there is no intercourse and no sympathy, who are as ignorant of each other's habits, thoughts and feelings as if they were dwellers of different zones, or inhabitants of different planets.[80]

Habyarimana's coup and the politics of the '70s and '80s

General Juvenal Habyarimana took power from Kayibanda in a coup during July 1973. At the time, Rwandan elites welcomed his action as an end to the factional politics and infighting that had paralyzed Kayibanda's government during its waning years.[81] Habyarimana allowed

Tutsi to continue working in the private sector and barred physical attacks against them, but retained Kayibanda's Hutuist ideology and barred Tutsi from positions of political power.[82] He was equally firm with the Hutu political opposition. In an interview with a French journalist he candidly confessed, "I know some people favor multipartyism, but as far as I am concerned, I have had no hesitation in choosing the single party system."[83] In 1974 he created the Mouvement Révolutionnaire National pour le Développement (MRND) and instituted it as the state's sole party. Electoral mandates of 99.98% kept Habyarimana in power.[84]

Habyarimana muted political life and focused on stability realized through social and economic development. Rwanda rose from second to last in a 1962 ranking of the world's per-capita poorest countries to 18th up from the bottom in 1987, on par with China. The service sector and export agriculture—coffee and tea—expanded at a healthy clip through the mid-1980s, and the rising prosperity allowed health and education programs to make themselves felt in the countryside.[85] Rwanda's new-found reputation for order and, particularly rare in East Africa, honest government, enabled it to became a major foreign aid recipient as donors shied away from Amin's Uganda, socialist Tanzania, "Tutsi apartheid" in Burundi, and Mobutu's kleptocratic Zaire.[86] The historian Gerard Prunier describes Rwanda between the 1970s and mid-1980s as, "carefully controlled, clean and in good order. The peasants were hard working, clean living....There was almost no crime…"[87] The legacy of this period has survived today in the form of buffet-lunches at Kigali's smarter restaurants, a legacy, one is told, of a Habyarimana edict instructing government employees to take shorter lunch breaks.

Rwanda's tranquility began to break down in the late 1980s. World coffee and tin prices—Rwanda's two principal exports—collapsed, depriving elites of their income and straining inter-elite relations.[88] The World Bank and donor nations pressed for a structural adjustment program that dealt a second blow to elites and peasants already suffering from commodity price declines.[89] A drought in 1989, coupled with evidence of rising corruption, prompted the domestic opposition to renew demands for democratic change.[90] In July 1990, Habyarimana waffled, agreeing to create a commission to study democratization but making no clear promises.[91] For the first time in 15 years, Rwanda's government was looking less than wholly secure.

Against this instability, on October 1, 1990 the Rwandan Patriotic Front invaded from Uganda. Understanding Rwandan history since that date requires that we turn to the exile communities established by those who fled the rise of Hutu dominance.

The RPF Invasion and Civil War

The refugees of the Rwandan diaspora—the hundreds of thousands who had fled beginning in 1959—never lost an emotional attachment to the nation of their birth. Even those who returned after the RPF victory in 1994 grow distant and introspective when asked to reflect on their lives as exiles and dreams of return.

The UN in late 1959 established large refugee camps in Uganda and Tanzania to host those escaping the violence across the Rwandan border. As the years progressed, many of these "Banyarwanda" left the camps to once again test their luck in the world. Some bought land and cattle to resume their traditional pastoral lifestyle, while others took professional positions with companies and NGOs from Bujumbura to New York.[92] Exile cohesion remained strong, aided in part by the lively Rwandan cultural associations that took root in cities with significant Banyarwanda populations.[93]

Uganda, host to the largest number of refugees, became the center of diaspora activity. In 1979, Banyarwanda leaders in Kampala established the Rwandese Alliance for National Unity (RANU), an organization immediately dedicated to helping Rwandan victims of Idi Amin but with a longer-term goal of facilitating refugees' return to Rwanda.[94]

RANU's stay in Kampala was brief, as the changing political winds that brought Milton Obote to power drove it to a quiescent exile-from-exile in Nairobi. Other exiles, however, took a more militant stand against Obote's repression. Thousands enlisted with Yoweri Museveni's anti-Obote guerrilla movement, and helped him fight his way from the bush to Kampala in 1986.[95] Two in particular, Major-General Fred Rwigyema and Colonel Paul Kagame, were old Museveni allies and quickly rose to senior positions—both became top commanders of the Ugandan national army Museveni established after assuming power.[96]

Banyarwanda drew two lessons from this experience in Uganda. Rising Banyarwanda power suggested to many that Uganda (and other nations) might offer a new national home. A 1988 diaspora conference in Washington, D.C., for example, recommended that refugees either naturalize in their country of residence or await a negotiated return to Rwanda.[97]

A minority of Banyarwanda drew a different lesson from their experience in the Ugandan bush. RANU's return to Kampala in late 1986 was a rallying cry to men who took the attitude "If the NRM [Museveni's army] could liberate Uganda, [we] began to ask why [we] could not to the same in Rwanda."[98] In 1987 they rechristened RANU the Rwandan Patriotic Front (RPF) and vowed that armed struggle was the only road home.[99]

Acceptance in Uganda proved illusory. Questions of Banyarwanda loyalty in the years following Museveni's victory reduced exile power in Uganda's armed forces. Even respected officers found their positions precarious, and increasingly contemplated using their military prowess to return to Rwanda.[100] But it was political changes of a different sort that turned this discontent into action.

Since the 1960s, Banyarwanda refugees in southern Uganda had been leaving the refugee camps and squatting on adjacent ranchland. By the late 1980s tensions over land rights had developed into a minor political crisis. A government commission appointed in 1988 to resolve squatter-landlord disputes advocated substantial land redistribution.[101] Such a program was a legal possibility—the ranchers were leasing the land from the government though a series of sweetheart deals—but a bitter pill politically.[102] In August of 1990 the ranchers rebelled. Museveni sent in troops to restore order, but each field victory represented a political loss as ranchers accused the government of favoring refugees at the expense of native Ugandans.[103] Intensifying political pressure forced the Ugandan leader to reinstate discriminatory policies linking citizenship to indigeneity, and to pledge that "only Ugandan citizens will be the beneficiaries of [any] ranching schemes."[104]

   This anti-Banyarwanda decision dealt a severe blow to the integrationist faction of the Rwandan exile community while raising the prestige of those who advocated military action against Habyarimana. RPF officers organized and quickly drafted plans for an invasion of Rwanda; Museveni offered covert support on condition that there be no return.[105]

   On the night of September 30, 1990 some 4,000 Banyarwanda soldiers of the Ugandan National Resistance Army (NRA) abandoned their barracks under the cloak of night and headed south for a rendezvous near the Uganda-Rwanda border. The following day, October 1, the Rwandese Patriotic Front crossed the border and launched its first attack on Rwandan soil.[106] For the militant exile community, the long-anticipated return had begun.

   Habyarimana's forces dealt swift, devastating blows to the attackers during the first few days of fighting. According to Professor Mahmood Mamdani, "by any reckoning, [the attack] was a failure."[107] Only after RPF Major Paul Kagame cut short a military training program in the United States and reorganized the RPF fighters into an effective guerilla force did the war's prevailing winds begin to shift.[108]

A tall, reed-thin, angular-looking man, Kagame first rose to prominence as a close associate of Museveni during their time in the Ugandan bush. The guerrilla tactics he honed during that protracted campaign served Kagame well in this new war. By mid-1991, he secured positions in Rwanda's Virunga Mountains and was launching ever deeper raids into the country.[109]

Habyarimana's initial reaction to the RPF attack was opportunistic. He quickly cracked down on his domestic opposition, eventually taking 13,000 people into custody.[110] In the international arena, Habyarimana exploited French fears of Anglophone perfidy—the RPF, like their Ugandan allies, are English speaking—to secure military assistance in the form of troops and advisors.[111] Several observers have argued that this French assistance bolstered Habyarimana's confidence and encouraged him to escalate of violence.[112] Finally, he used Hutu fears of RPF intentions to consolidate his popular support. Government propagandists warned that the RPF planned to re-establish an absolutist Tutsi monarchy and urged that Hutu protest the invasion with slogans like "Let slavery, servitude and discord be finished forever!"[113] Extremists in government, who controlled the publication *Kangura,* issued more dire warnings. By early 1991, articles and leaflets made reference to a Tutsi war that that planned "a genocide, the extermination of the Hutu majority."[114] Even domestic Tutsi found themselves under attack by government officials who dredged up old conspiratorial notions of Tutsi unity. The Minister of Justice, for example, declared "that the Tutsi were *ibyitso,* 'accomplices' of the invaders," and warned that "to prepare an attack [on the scale of the RPF invasion] required trusted people [on the inside.] Rwandans of the same ethnic group," he continued, "offered that possibility better than did others."[115] This rhetoric may have temporarily shored up Habyarimana's government, but at the expense of ethnic harmony.

A military stalemate prevailed throughout 1991. Domestic political activists, sensing that the war had weakened the Habyarimana's regime, ignored the threat of arrest and stepped up calls for democracy.[116] Under pressure both at home and from donors abroad, on July 5, 1991 Habyarimana reluctantly announced democratic reforms.

A dozen new parties sprouted up overnight.[117] Some were genuinely oppositional, but others were Habyarimana-managed sham parties created to give the appearance of pluralism without reducing the President's power.[118] Following Habyarimana's own lead, many turned to ethnic rhetoric as a tool for gaining popular support.[119] More troubling still was a trend of establishing quasi-military youth wings that turned politics into bloodshed. The most notorious of these groups was the ruling MRND's Interahamwe, which began murdering Tutsi in March 1992.[120]

A new, pluralist cabinet was sworn in on the April 7, 1992.[121] Although Habyarimana's MRND controlled the key Defense, Civil Service, Interior and Transport Ministries, in July the opposition stole the political initiative by meeting with RPF representatives in Brussels. On June 6, the RPF agreed to cease its armed struggle and participate in peace talks in Arusa, Tanzania, scheduled later that year.

Negotiations ran from September 1992 through early 1993, hammering out agreements on power sharing and a reorganized military that included RPF soldiers.[122] But these official peace negotiations masked hard-liner moves towards war. Hutu extremists within the military developed social networks, funneled aid to party militias, and may have begun to develop plans for genocide.[123] They also established Rwanda's infamous "hate radio"—Radio Télévision Libre des Milles Collines (RTLM)—and began its inflammatory, relentlessly divisive broadcasts.[124]

Sporadic political violence in early 1993 prompted the RPF to renew hostilities in the name of preserving order. On February 8, its forces invaded the area near Byumba, in the north of Rwanda. The attack was immediately successful and by mid-February RPF troops were a scant 30 kilometers north of Kigali. French pressure on the RPF, however, spared Habyarimana further defeats and forced the two parties back to the negotiating table.[125] The resulting Arusha Accords established a multiethnic government and guaranteed opposition parties significant representation in the national Cabinet. The Rwandan army was reorganized with a 60/40 numerical division between government and RPF forces. Senior officer positions were divided equally.[126]

Rwanda's economy was in shambles. Inflation and public debt were soaring, while export earnings and per capita income plunged.[127] Economic decline heightened domestic tensions but also conspired to raise the relative power of donor nations, who used the "ultimate threat" of an aid embargo to wrench a signature from Habyarimana's hand on August 4, 1993 despite hard-liner opposition.[128] Superficially, at least, peace was at hand.

The Arusha peace began to unravel a mere month after it began. A Tutsi-sponsored coup in neighboring Burundi murdered the popular Hutu President Melchior Ndadaye, confirming, in the minds of Hutu extremists, the relentless drive of Tutsi political ambitions.[129] Propagandists exploited the tragedy to inflame Hutu passions against Rwandan Tutsi, and the well-connected government hardliners established the "Hutu Power" movement to promote Hutu supremacy. Political rallies denounced Tutsi as irreconcilably opposed to majority rule and urged Hutu solidarity. Physical attacks against Tutsi were tacitly promoted.[130]

The first months of 1994 spun out of control. Political militias and in some cases government officials distributed machetes and other weapons to the population. Political violence increased still further, and there were worrying signs that it was directed by hardliners within government.[131] On April 4, President Habyarimana flew to Dar es Salaam for a regional conference, called to discuss enforcement of the Arusha accords. Rumor had it that neighboring heads of State were going to pressure the Rwandan leader into clamping down on violence and ethnic rhetoric, but the world will never know what Habyarimana took from that meeting.[132] As his spotless French jet flew low into the Kigali airport on the evening of April 6, a missile went up from a nearby hill and destroyed the plane. Habyarimana died instantly, and within hours the Hutu-extremist Théoneste Bagosora formed a government bent on genocide.[133]

Killings of Tutsi and Bagosora's Hutu opponents began within hours of Habyarimana's death. Some witnesses remember seeing roadblocks before they heard the explosion of the Presidential plane, lending credence to the theory that Habyarimana's own power-hungry subordinates killed him.[134]

At first, the violence was orderly. Lists of the new regime's political opponents in the capital were distributed to military and militia units, who systematically hunted them down. By April 7, targeted killings of prominent Tutsi began in provincial cities while rumors spread like wildfire through the countryside.[135]

Sometime before April 11, the government appears to have decided to go ahead with its "final solution," a general genocide of the Tutsi. The political militias—particularly the MRND's Interahamwe, some 50,000 strong nationwide—were mobilized and placed under command of loyal government officials.[136] Killers searched door-to-door for Tutsi and quickly threw up roadblocks to catch those who trying to escape.[137] The scope of the violence widened throughout April as Bagosora's government consolidated power and replaced those government officials—such as Prefect Habyalimana in Butare—who initially used their influence to prevent ethnic violence.[138] By late April the growing piles of corpses were becoming a major health crisis as well as a political embarrassment in the international arena.

The killing spread in the context of a renewed civil war. Sensing the imminent genocide, the RPF withdrew from government on April 8 and restarted its military campaign. The RPF scored early victories in the field. Its forces reached the outskirts of Kigali on April 11, and laid siege to the city and just as the tempo of death rose. Other RPF divisions struck west towards Tanzania. By mid-May, the RPF had captured substantial territory in the northeast near the Ugandan border and around Kigali—though the city itself remained under government control.[139]

The civil war provided ammunition for the rhetoric of genocide. Hysterical RTLM and Radio Rwanda announcers urged the Hutu to close ranks and kill Tutsi for fear of being exterminated by the invaders. No discrimination was made between exiles and domestic Tutsi. One RTLM broadcast, for example, urged:

> Courage! Don't wait for the armed forces to intervene. Act fast and don't allow these enemies to continue their advance! If you wait for the authorities, that's your problem. They are not the ones who are going to look out for your houses during the night! You must defend yourselves.[140]

There is evidence that the genocide's pace fluctuated in response to RPF victories, implying that at least some organizers saw murder as a form of deterrence or revenge.[141] This was certainly the view of some killers, who express little or no guilt over their actions. As one 74-year old later killer put it, "Either you took part in the massacre or else you were massacred yourself. So I took weapons and defended the members of my tribe against the Tutsi."[142]

Government and Interahamwe officials used both promises and threats to encourage broader public participation. Killers were sometimes granted the land or cattle of their victims, while those who refused risked becoming victims themselves.[143] The killing itself seemed wholly irrational. One UN officer remarked, "I had seen war before, but I had never seen a woman carrying a baby on her back kill another woman with a baby on her back."[144] Killers would sometimes spare or even hide Tutsi friends while indiscriminately killing those they did not know.[145] 2

By June, the genocidal regime was breathing its last. The RFP had secured much of Rwanda's north, and the French were finally spurred into sending a humanitarian force, *Opération Turquoise*, into the south.[146] The RPF took Kigali in early July, and launched a final push to expel genocidal members of the old regime sill holding out in the northwest. The RPF's victory was total. By August 1, it had defeated all remnants of the Habyarimana regime, halted the genocidal killing and installed itself as Rwanda's national government.

Estimates of the numbers killed in the genocide vary widely, but even the low-end figures are horrifying. The UN's official estimate in November 1994 was 500,000, out of a pre-genocide population of 7.7 million.[147] Professor Gérard Prunier, who worked with the French government in 1994, contrasted data from an August 1991 census with post-genocide counts of Tutsi to arrive at a widely cited 800–850,000 deaths.[148] A not-yet published Rwandan government report that includes deaths between October 1990 and the end of 1994 estimates 1.07 million deaths, and that 94% of the victims were Tutsi.[149] None of these figures include those killed during 1996 RPF incursions into Zairian refugee camps, which may add over 100,000 to the toll.[150]

Numbers of genocidaires are equally staggering. The RPF government adopted a policy of arresting almost anyone accused of participating, and those taken into custody soon overwhelmed both prisons and courts. Ten thousand suspects had been arrested by November of 1994, a number which reached 86,000 in 1996 and currently stands at over 120,000.[151] While 15 percent of those may be innocent, victims of bad luck or covetous neighbors, an additional estimated 30,000 to 60,000 genocidaires remain free.[152]

---

2.   Scott Strauss, a University of California-Berkeley graduate student writing his dissertation on Rwanda, argues that sparing friends was a common motive for killing strangers. Hutu could hide Tutsi without raising public suspicions so long as they appeared outwardly zealous about the genocide.

Refugee numbers were no more heartening. The RPF victory touched off three massive human migrations. The first began in early July when nearly two million Hutu, 30 percent of Rwanda's population, fled first to parts of Rwanda not yet under RPF control and then across the border into squalid UN camps in the Congo and Tanzania.[153] Some of these refugees were government officials or Interahamwe members fearing revenge, but many others left because the soon-to-be-deposed Hutu government had warned of an impending RPF genocide of the Hutu. Conversely, Tutsi exiles returned en masse to RPF-ruled Rwanda. The government estimates that 750,000 returned by the end of 1995.[154] Many of these returnees had either last seen Rwanda as young children or were born abroad, and found themselves coming "home" to a country with a culture quite foreign from the ones in which they were raised. Finally, in 1996 RPF-backed Zairian rebels shut the refugee camps, prompting nearly a million Hutu to return home to Rwanda.[155]

These statistics on deaths and refugees caused many to label Rwanda—along with Somalia and Bosnia—a "failed state." Few saw how anything resembling a viable nation could emerge from these ruins of 1994.

The Genocide's Legacy

Today, all physical traces of the genocide have been eradicated from Kigali's leafy streets and the prettily cultivated hills of Rwanda's countryside. Gaping holes have been left in one side of the Parliament building as a memorial, but they appear so out of place in the rebuilt capital that most foreign visitors pause before realizing the damage was due to 1994 shelling. Hotels, restaurants, and new houses have sprung up in the capitol, and, to a lesser extent, in the provinces. Walking by bougainvillea-draped walls or enjoying a drink in Kigali's fashionable Embassy district, it is quite possible to momentarily forget Rwanda's recent past.

Politically, too, Rwanda has stabilized. Guerilla incursions by Hutu rebel groups based in the Congo largely petered out by the late 1990s. Although one notices a heavy security presence throughout the country, there is no sense of insecurity. The RPF held the country's first post-genocide municipal elections in 1999 and has pledged further democratization with national elections tentatively scheduled in late 2003.[156] Human rights groups do report sporadic attacks on government critics, several of whom have fled abroad, but the RPF's level of political repression is certainly below that used by its predecessor.[157]

The relative wealth of Kigali, however, tends to mask rural poverty. The RPF's encouragement of international investment and NGO-run economic development programs has restored the economy to pre-1994 levels and achieved a 6 percent growth rate in 2001, but the country remains highly dependent on subsistence farming and has a per capita income of under $300.[158] The functional literacy rate is at most 50 percent, and fewer than that have access to sanitary water.[159] Government budgets are tight and depend on foreign aid to cover about 30 percent of outlays. As a result, prison, justice, and reparations expenses must compete for resources with development projects and vitally needed social services.

The veneer of normalcy also masks the genocide's understandably deep and pernicious impact on ethnic relations. Mutual distrust persists. Tutsi, both the rescappés (survivors) and returnees, remain suspicious of their Hutu neighbors and fear that democratization's inevitable restoration of Hutu rule will mark a return to oppression or even violence. They also want justice. Hutu, conversely, are suspicious of the RPF government. They view it as an autocratic extension of the Tutsi *mwami* and fear that RPF justice will take the form of revenge.

RPF violence in the Congo and memories of Habyarimana's propaganda during the civil war have hardened the Hutu belief that both sides were equally responsible for the genocide. In this context, Rwanda's imprisonment of 120,000 suspected Hutu genocidaires has had a deleterious effect on ethnic relations. Hutu families see themselves deprived of their primary wage earners and think that reluctance to prosecute Tutsi suspected of atrocities and the slow pace of justice prove RPF perfidy. The Tutsi, in turn, perceive Hutu suspicions of justice as lack of remorse for Tutsi suffering.

Tensions are compounded by patterns of Rwandan settlement. Most Rwandans live in ethnically mixed small villages where victims are daily forced to cross paths with genocidaires or their families. They are required to share public buildings, water supplies, and common pastures, and to work together in local government. The occasional talk of creating a "Hutuland" and "Tutsiland" would require forcibly displacing hundreds of thousands of Rwandans who have already suffered amply. Separation is not a possibility. As a consequence, justice and reconciliation are necessary for enduring stability

2

JUSTICE FOR RADICAL EVIL[160]

○ ○

I don't understand what reconciliation would mean unless some of those responsible were brought to justice

—Paul Kagame

The Rwandan Patriotic Front came to power promising to punish those who had killed. Its leadership saw justice both as a moral duty to the survivors and as necessary for reconciliation.[161] As people began to recognize the full scope of the genocide and the staggering numbers of deaths and killers, RPF leaders increasingly stated that the goal of justice was to end "the culture of impunity" that allowed such killings.[162]

The genocide's destruction of the country, however, hindered the government's ability to prosecute those responsible for it. Only 14 public prosecutors and 39 criminal investigators survived the genocide, and more than two-thirds of the nation's judges had been killed or fled.[163] Court buildings and administrative offices were ransacked or destroyed, the only functional vehicles belonged to RPF military units, and essential office supplies like pens and paper were nonexistent.[164] By early August, RPF leadership realized that more than a hundred thousand cases might overwhelm its limited judicial capacity.[165]

The resolute RPF persisted despite these obstacles. In March 1995, it announced that the first prosecutions would take place to mark the 1-year anniversary of the genocide.[166] Prosecutors technically achieved this goal by entering charges against 6 suspects in a Kigali court on April 7th, but the presiding judge indefinitely postponed the cases to allow more time to collect evidence.[167]

Rwandan justice did not begin in earnest for another year and a half. On August 30, 1996 the Rwandan Parliament passed Organic Law No. 8/96 establishing a dozen specialized chambers within the Tribunals of First Instance and military courts whose sole purpose is to hear cases stemming from the genocide. By that time substantial international assistance had allowed the country to rebuild its judicial and prosecutorial infrastructure, but the pace of justice remained slow and procedural safeguards weak—the Rwandan government declared itself unable to pay for defendants' legal representation.[168] That declaration, and the charged political climte, prompted numerous international aid groups to express concern that the trials would not be fair. Subsequent years have witnessed some improvement in the situation. Almost 6,000 people have been tried. International NGOs such as Lawyers without Borders have assisted by providing defense attorneys, and the acquittal rate has been between 15 and 20 percent.[169]

RPF plans for justice were paralleled on the global stage by the developing International Criminal Tribunal for Rwanda (ICTR). UN Security Council Resolution 955 established the Tribunal on November 8, 1994, and a resolution the following February seated it in Arusha.

Security Council Resolution 955 gives the ICTR jurisdictional primacy over national courts. From the beginning, the ICTR saw its mission as prosecuting planners of the genocide while leaving their subordinates to face Rwandan justice.[170] This jurisdictional primacy, the Tribunal's location in Tanzania, and the absence of capital sentences have all made for a cool relationship between the RPF and the ICTR.

The ICTR has fared no better than Rwanda's domestic courts. Rwanda's post-genocide destruction proved as much a hindrance to ICTR investigators as to their national counterparts, and Arusha's distance from the scene of the genocide further slowed investigations. The ICTR did not hold its first cases until mid-1996. It has since indicted 61 individuals, and has or is trying several dozen of those.

The Liberal-Prosecutorial Model of Transitional Justice

The fact that these prosecutions seem a natural response to Rwanda's genocide masks the relative novelty of transitional justice. Prior to the Allied trials of Nazi leaders at Nuremburg, senior members of defeated regimes expected pardons, exile, or speedy execution for any crimes they committed while serving as heads of state. None could have imagined that victorious opponents would throw the book at them.[1]

Even after Nuremburg, Cold War politicking threatened to turn the World War II prosecutions into remarkable one-time events. Of the democratic transitions in southern Europe in the 1970s, only Constantine Karamanlis' government in Greece prosecuted former leaders for human rights crimes.[171] Truth commissions emerged in the 1980s as much of Latin America joined the rising "third wave" of democratic transitions, but criminal accountability remained rare.[172] Indeed, despite the Geneva Convention, the Genocide Convention and other treaties, only since the early 1990s has Nuremburg taken root as a pre-

---

1. Gary Bass' recent book *Stay the Hand of Vengeance* traces the roots of modern war-crimes trials to the close of the Napoleonic Wars, and certainly the idea of prosecuting disagreeable world leaders pre-dates World War II. But British, Franch and Russian efforts to prosecute the Turks responsible for the Armenian genocide are illustrative of the chilly reception international diplomats gave such ideas prior to Nuremburg: "political compromises were reached, the impetus for such trials dissipated and the Armenian massacre became the 'forgotten genocide' of the twentieth century." (Antonio Cassese, "Reflections on International Criminal Justice. 2).

cedent in international law. The first international criminal tribunal since 1945 was created in 1993, with jurisdiction over crimes committed in Yugoslavia. The UN established the ICTR the following year, and in early 2002 it authorized a similar tribunal for Sierra Leone.

This trend towards prosecuting former leaders for crimes they committed against their own people is growing, and is reflected by the building momentum for an International Criminal Court (ICC). The idea of a standing international tribunal empowered to try human rights crimes originated after WWII, but the recent push began in 1989 when Trinidad and Tobago suggested that such a body could prove helpful in combating international drug trafficking.[173] In the mid-1990s, the International Law Commission and *ad hoc* working committees developed a statutory basis for the ICC. The effort culminated with a 1998 conference in Rome that overwhelmingly ratified the so-called Rome Statute for the International Criminal Court, to become effective after ratification by 60 signatories.[174] The current count is 56.[175]

Several states' domestic law also evinces acceptance this trend. Rwanda provides the clearest example of this, but prosecutions have been contemplated in Chile, South Africa—where those who refuse the Truth and Reconciliation Commission's offer of amnesty are liable to criminal sanction—and elsewhere. Belgium has given its courts universal jurisdiction over human rights crimes, and several Rwandans have been convicted in its courts. The Alien Tort Claims Act of 1789 and Torture Victim Protection Act of 1991 grant victims of human rights crimes more limited rights to sue for damages in American courts. Even Senegalese courts initiated action against former Chadian dictator Hissene Habré, although a judge later ordered him freed.

These legal developments—combined with a burgeoning literature on transitional justice—present the outlines of an emergent dominant model, which I term the liberal-prosecutorial model of transitional justice. This model increasingly guides global efforts to prosecute those state officials responsible for crimes against their own people.

There are three components to the liberal-prosecutorial model of transitional justice: (1) the international prosecution of the "planners and organizers" of state-sponsored crimes; (2) domestic prosecution of their subordinates; and (3) an investigatory truth commission to write an official history of a regime's crimes and to illustrate the behavior of broad societal sectors—such as health, business, and journalism—that contributed *as sectors* to a state's crimes but which are too diffuse to face criminal sanction.

International prosecutions have preemptory jurisdiction, for several reasons.[2] International judges are presumed to be less biased and better qualified to interpret violations of international law than their national counterparts.[3] Practically speaking, international prosecutions may be a more realistic option than national ones given frequent state resistance to trials, and international prosecutors will be free of the political

---

2.   International primacy is the most controversial tenet of this liberal-prosecutorial model. Neil Kritz, for example, writes, "This automatic preference for international responses should be resisted." (Kritz, "Coming to Terms With Atrocities." 145.) The Rome Statute makes concessions to domestic courts by providing that it "shall be complementary to national criminal jurisdictions" (Part 1, Article 1) and by stipulating that cases are inadmissible if "The case is being investigated or prosecuted by a State which has jurisdiction over it, unless the State is unwilling or unable genuinely to carry out the investigation or prosecution." (Part 2, Article 17, Section 1(a)) However, this final stipulation demonstrates the inherent primacy of international jurisdiction because (1) the ICC is responsible for determining cases where "the state is unwilling or unable" to prosecute; and (2) the threat of ICC pre-emption of a case effectively forces domestic prosecutors to investigate and prosecute in accordance with international law. Furthermore, states are preempted from trying in domestic courts cases already judged by the ICC in domestic courts. (Mark Drumbl, "Punishment, Postgenocide: From Guilt to Shame to Civis in Rwanda." 38.

3.   Professor B.V.A. Roling once wrote, "For the very reason that war crimes are violations of the laws of war, that is of international law, an international judge should try the international offences. He is the best qualified." (Cited in Antonio Cassese, "Reflections on International Criminal Justice. 7).

pressures that sometimes hinder domestic investigations.[176] National court jurisdiction of foreign crimes, as with Belgium's Universal Jurisdiction law, is at best a stopgap measure until the appropriate international forums are developed.

The South African Truth and Reconciliation Commission's idea of offering "amnesty for truth" evoked a great deal of excitement in the international legal community, but the weight of opinion appears to favor prosecuting at least those individuals at the top of a criminal regime. For example, former ICTY judge Antonio Cassese writes, "the best option is to bring to court alleged culprits and to dispense justice" because "appalling atrocities…are beyond amnesty" and because of warring parties' reluctance to be reconciled.[177] Truth Commissions are complementary to prosecutions but can serve as a second-best option applicable when political realities preempt justice.

In this model, defendants are to be tried in adversarial courts and accorded the civil rights which Western citizens take for granted and which are enshrined in the *Universal Declaration of Human Rights,* the *International Covenant on Civil and Political Rights,* and other authoritative international legal texts. This is true regardless of whether defendants are tried by international tribunals or national courts. David Crocker, for example, writes:

> Transitional societies should comply with the rule of law…. The rule of law includes respect for due process, in the sense of procedural fairness, publicity, and impartiality. Like cases must be treated alike, *ex post facto* laws eschewed, and private revenge prohibited.[178]

Likewise, defendants are to be protected against cruel or unusual punishment. Prison terms are the default punishment of the existing international tribunals, though some states (including Rwanda) would like to see capital penalties.

The liberal-prosecutorial model of transitional justice arose out of a particular type of transitional situation—democratization—and from the efforts of democratic successor regimes to hold their predecessors accountable for a certain class of crime, which Professor Jose Alvarez has termed "crimes of states." "Crimes of states" are human rights violations that either benefit from the complicity of a state government or are direct functions of state policy.[179] They are carried out by relatively few people in comparison to the number of victims or the population as a whole. Crimes of states often (but not always) violate existing laws are by and large committed secretly—though the secret may be open—because those responsible for them know that many would see their acts as deeply immoral. Latin America's disappearances, or on a grander scale Hitler's massacre of the Jews,[4] are the paradigmatic crimes of states. The officials responsible for these crimes of states acted with horrific impunity, but needed plausible deniability for their actions.

The basis of liberal-prosecutorial justice in such situations is twofold: moral and utilitarian.[5] Justice in states recovering from "crimes of states" is seen as a moral duty arising from a liberal conception of human rights, and of utilitarian benefit to both the transitional regime and the larger international order. The common utilitarian arguments can be summarized as follows, and I will elaborate on each one below:

1. Prosecution is necessary to assert the supremacy of democratic values and norms and to encourage the public to believe in them.

2. Prosecution is essential to establish the viability of the democratic system. If the military and police establishments can prevent prosecution through political influence or the threat of a

---

4. Though much of Nazi Germany's early anti-Semitism was legal.
5. I recognize that utilitarian ethicists may take issue with this dichotomy. However, I intend the distinction only to differentiate metaphysical and deontological rationales from outcome-oriented ones. It is in no way intended as a critique of utilitarian morality.

coup, democracy does not really exist in the country, and the struggle to establish democracy must go on.[180]

3.   Prosecution is necessary to establish the rule of law.[181]

4.   Prosecution is essential for deterrence: to prevent future atrocities elsewhere. Antonio Cassese cites Hitler's perhaps apocryphal quotation, spoken during deliberations over his 'final solution,' "Who, after all, speaks today of the annihilation of the Armenians?"[182]

5.   "Justice dissipates the call for revenge" and militates against renewed fighting.[183]

6.   It is a fiction to think that a people can forget a crime against humanity. Justice is required so that memory does not fester.[184]

7.   Trials, especially in conjunction with truth commissions, establish a historical record of a regime's atrocities so that the victims will live on in memory and future generations can understand their national past.[185] 6

8.   Trials reduce tensions after a conflict by establishing "individual responsibility over collective assignation of guilt."[186] Trials demonstrate that individual men, not "all Hutu" or "all Serbs," are murderers.

9.   Justice promotes reconciliation at both a personal and national level.

---

6.   Legal positivists argue also that prosecution is a duty required under international law. Diane Orentlicher, for example, writes that international law, codified in the Genocide Convention, the Convention against torture, the International Covenant on Civil and Political Rights, the European Convention for the Protection of Human Rights and Fundamental Freedoms, and the American Convention on Human Rights, among other treaties, specifies a duty to prosecute and punish the most egregious violators of human rights. (Diane Orentlicher, "Settling Accounts." 383–416.)

Arguments One and Two turn on transitional justice's ability to consolidate democracy. At a very basic level, prosecuting (presumably anti-democratic) former government officials weakens them by imprisoning or otherwise removing them from positions of vestigial power. From a public perspective, the trials conclusively demonstrate a decisive break with the past, and show that the new leaders are not merely new faces for the same old powerbrokers. Conversely, "failing to prosecute may generate in the populace cynicism and distrust towards the political system."[187] More significantly still, some analysts argue that prosecution of crimes of states is essential to building the strong civil society required for effective democratic governance. Laurence Whitehead, for example, writes that unless crimes are "investigated and punished, there can be no real growth of trust, no 'implanting' of democratic norms in society at large, and therefore no genuine 'consolidation' of democracy."[188]

Argument Three, that prosecution is necessary to promote the rule of law, takes several forms. Ruti Teitel reminds us of the distinction between rule-of-law as legal continuity—a meaning that requires transitional courts to respect even the unjust laws of the old regime and to refuse *ex post facto* prosecutions—and rule-of-law as equality before the law and substantive justice.[189] Teitel argues for the latter interpretation, which lends itself to justifications of prosecution by making reference to natural law theory.[190] A positivist alternative is to derive a duty to prosecute from international legal precedents.

Rule of law as equality before the law and substantive justice benefits society by guarding against arbitrary state actions and guaranteeing political rights. Failing to hold members of the former regime accountable, on the other hand, perpetuates their feeling of impunity and "may vitiate the authority of law itself."[191] We are admonished to remember William Pitt's dictum, "Where law ends, tyranny begins."[192]

The fourth argument, deterrence, is the most commonly articulated justification for prosecuting human rights criminals. Dianne Orentlicher is hardly alone in writing that, "The fulcrum of the case for criminal punishment is that it is the most effective insurance against future repression. By laying bare the truth about violations of the past and condemning them, prosecutions can deter potential lawbreakers and inoculate the public against future temptation to be complicit in state sponsored violence."[193]

The deterrence argument takes two forms: international and domestic. International prosecutions of state officials in particular are thought to have a deterrent effect against authoritarian violations of human rights elsewhere. Even without forcible international intervention to halt an atrocity, the threat of international prosecution can deter by denying national leaders international aid, a comfortable exile (should his regime fall), and Western medical and banking services for himself and his family.

RPF justifications for prosecuting Rwanda's genocidaires offer a paradigmatic example of deterrence theory applied to the domestic arena. RPF officials with some justification see the atrocities of 1994 as merely the most recent and egregious event in a line of officially sanctioned ethnic violence. These repeated attacks have had tragic consequences on the Rwandan psyche. Justice Minister Jean De Dieu Mucyo writes:

> The impunity that was long enjoyed by the authors of previous social dramas had resulted through the years in the trivialization of violations by Rwandan authorities and populations…Eradicating this impunity is a prerequisite for peaceful coexistence followed by social cohesion [and] implies the systematic capture, trial and sentencing of all those involved in the tragic events that plunged the country into mourning, without considering either their large number or the limited capacity of the country's justice system.[194]

Justice is required to eradicate the "culture of impunity" that allowed genocidaires to think their crimes would have no personal repercussions. Only prosecution and punishment for the crimes of 1994 can deter future ethnic violence.

Argument Five holds that prosecuting human rights criminals helps maintain domestic order by deterring revenge killings—certainly some prominent victims have historically hunted down and killed victimizers who had escaped justice.

Arguments Six and Seven hold that justice is necessary for memory. Cassese eloquently summarizes Six when he writes, "forgetting makes a mockery of the dead."[195] The second holds that "forgetting crimes against humanity and war crimes is, in any event a fiction."[196] Memories of injustice have a pernicious tendency to linger and, in the absence of justice, may renew conflicts.

Argument Eight on this list is that criminal accountability for atrocities can reduce tensions by assigning guilt to individuals rather than groups—e.g., justice will show Tutsi that not all Hutus are genocidaires.[197] Argument Nine holds more broadly that justice is a necessary precursor to reconciliation: victims presumably are more willing to forgive, or at least tolerate, wrongdoers who have faced justice and paid their dues. Reducing tensions, building trust, and promoting reconciliation are all seen essential for long-term stability.

Some of these arguments are more convincing than others. Although deterrence theory has an intuitive appeal, the historical record to date offers scant evidence of its efficacy. Nuremburg failed to deter the late 20th century's numerous bloody interstate wars, and atrocity has remained a depressingly routine part of civil war despite the ICTY and ICTR. Gary Bass, author of *Stay the Hand of Vengeance,* reminds us, "men willing to commit mass murder are terribly difficult to dissuade."[198]

There is, however, some reason to be more optimistic about the future. Transitional justice has historically been piecemeal. Prior to 1989, authoritarian leaders in much of the world knew that their respective Cold War patrons would preempt international prosecution of any state sponsored crimes. That protection has since been dramatically reduced.

Sociological studies—and, interestingly, computer models of human behavior—indicate groups of people can "tip" from criminality to honesty in startlingly short periods of time.[199] The risk-reward ratio for state-sponsored violence has historically been low, but elevating the risk (by, for example, establishing the ICC) might dissuade at least the more rational state officials from murderous actions.

Recent events in the Middle East are telling. Israeli Infrastructure Minister Avigdor Lieberman suggested during a March 2002 Cabinet meeting that the Israeli Defense Force should threaten the Palestinians by choosing a date and announcing, "At 8 a.m. we'll bomb all the [Palestinian] commercial centers. At noon we'll bomb their petrol stations. At 2 we'll bomb their banks." Shimon Perez' reply was, "And at 6 p.m. you'll receive an invitation to the international tribunal in The Hague."[200] International pressure would certainly have forced Israel to abandon the plan in any event, but Perez' statement may indicate that world leaders' fear of international prosecution is growing.

Domestic prosecutions, though more of a threat to subordinate participants in a state sponsored crime, carry substantial risks for a successor government. Argentine President Raul Alfonsin's efforts to try members of the deposed junta collapsed after a threatened coup.[201] Elsewhere, there is a widespread perception that threats of prosecution can slow democratic transitions.[202] Even if domestic prosecutions are a political possibility, they will likely have little deterrent effect abroad and may simply teach wrongdoers to fight harder—and keep clinging to power—next time.

The idea that justice is required for memory has an equally tenuous basis. Trials with their rules of procedure, extended time frame, and expense are inefficient mechanisms for writing history and often cannot capture the entire sweep of history. Truth commissions are better suited to this task.[203]

George Santayana's infamous quotation[7] aside, neither does forgetting past wrongdoing necessarily condemn men to future violence. Amnesties and collective amnesia have permitted numerous countries to bury their pasts while transitioning to peaceful, democratic futures. Memory, meanwhile, has a disheartening ability to reignite conflict.[8]

Whatever their relative merits, these utilitarian justifications for prosecution fundamentally aim at promoting human rights by ending the particular circumstances that give rise to crimes of states. Crimes of states are traditionally planned and orchestrated by a small elite that believes itself above the law and is prepared to use ruthless methods to maintain its power. Preventing similar crimes in the future therefore requires that a transitional regime eliminate the potential for such elites to capture power and then place themselves beyond the confines of morality and justice. The utilitarian justifications for prosecuting the

---

7.   Those who do not learn from the past are doomed to repeat it.

8.   Spain is the example par excellence of the successful use of an amnesty to overcome a legacy of human rights abuse. After winning the Spanish civil war, Franco and his agents machine-gunned an estimated 200,000 individuals between 1939 and 1943 and imprisoned 213,000 more. Though the repression grew milder towards the end of Franco's life, it continued throughout his years in power—between 1969 and 1974 alone, at least 500 union leaders and priests were arrested, and over 25,000 individuals lost their jobs for political activities. Following Franco's death in 1975, the Spanish government chose to neither prosecute or even investigate the human rights abuses of the Franco era. According to José María Maravall, the opposition groups negotiating with Franco's successor for a transition to democracy "had to renounce any policy of prosecution and punishment," as a precondition to the peaceful transition to a democratic regime. In 1976, King Juan Carlos granted a royal amnesty for many of the individuals convicted of political crimes under Franco, and in 1977 the new parliament voted for a blanket amnesty for all political crimes committed by the government and the opposition. At the time, newly elected Prime Minister Suárez commented, "The question is not to ask people where they are coming from, but where they are going to." Although Spain today is still plagued with an occasional ETA bombing, few today worry that Spain's choice to forget will doom it to decades of violence in the future. The amnesty appears to have permitted Spain to "move on" with its national life and put human rights crimes behind it.

former officials responsible for planning and executing crimes of states—promoting the rule of law, consolidating democracy, deterrence, memorializing evil—all aim to achieve this end. I will posit later that different transitional circumstances may need justice to accomplish different ends.

Several theorists endorse the Spanish model of an outright, blanket amnesty as a forward-looking, effective method of rebuilding a shattered society. Fernando Rodrigo, for example, argues that the first duty of a new regime is "to liberate people from their past in order to promote reconciliation and partnership." Doing otherwise simply reopens old wounds and re-ignites old conflicts in a country that needs peace and stability above all else.

The "those who forget the past are doomed to repeat it" argument opposing amnesties grows even more tenuous if we examine countries afflicted with what might be termed an overdose of historical memory. Vivid collective memories of past crimes that were never brought to justice may actually lend support the thesis that "Those who *remember* the past are doomed to repeat it." In Yugoslavia in the 1990s, leaders such as Milosevich and Tudjman skillfully used carefully parsed versions of history to fuel a nationalist fire of violence and repression, killing at a minimum tens of thousands of individuals and displacing hundreds of thousands of others. When the Yugoslavian wars began in 1991, Balkan fighters ended forty years of relative peace, stirred by references to history and Milosevich's pledge to Kosovo Serbs that despite a legacy of being second class citizens in the largely Albanian region, they "will not be beaten again." To be sure, these national leaders conjured up misleading and one-sided memories of the past and grossly perverted history to their own destructive ends. But in the Balkans, it was not forgetfulness of past atrocities that committed the region to a decade of violence. Memories did.

(This footnote was originally written for my Fall 2001 Junior Paper, supervised by Jonathan Allen.)

(The Spanish history is drawn from Anthony Beevor, The Spanish Civil War. (London, Orbis Publishing: 1982); Neil Kritz, editor, Transitional Justice: Volume II (Country Studies). (Washington, United States Institute of Peace Press: 1995); and Mary Albon, *Project on Justice in Times of Transition: Report of the Project's Inaugural Meeting*, in Neil Kritz (editor), Transitional Justice: Volume 1 (General Considerations). (Washington, United States Institute of Peace Press: 1995). The Yugoslavian history comes from BBC Documentary Films, *Yugoslavia: Death of a Nation.*

Such utilitarian concerns, however, are only half of the foundation for the liberal-prosecutorial model of transitional justice. The liberal notion that human beings are right-possessing entities and that right-violators must be punished is a strong if sometimes unstated undercurrent in the debate. This liberal belief in human rights can justify prosecuting wrongdoers in two ways: deontological retributivism and contractual retributivism.

G.W.F. Hegel's writings have influenced the deontological retributivist view, though, as one philosopher writes, "That Hegel expounded a justification of punishment is clear. The type, logic, and details of his justification, however, are less clear."[204] Hegel's justification of punishment derives from his larger metaphysical conception of "Abstract Right," a concept similar to Locke's state of nature, "except that its beings are not natural men but abstract persons, with not natural rights but abstract rights."[205] Hegel saw crime as an expressive act that not only deprives a victim of property (or wellbeing) but also denies the victim's capacity for rights in general.[206] "Crime," writes one interpreter, "involves the coercing of the innocent person's will and therefore the denial (or negation) of the freedom and rights of the victim's will."[207] Hegel further maintained that a criminal denial of an individual's free will is simultaneously a denial of the very idea of free will because all men are equal in their possession of it.[208] Free will (and rights), however, exist. Therefore, the criminal's denial of free will must be punished as a way of affirming and continuing free will's existence.[209]

In short, Hegel saw punishment as the necessary logical result of any rational belief in human rights. To quote one of David Cooper's influential essays on Hegel, "Unless people are generally apprehended and punished for preventing others doing *x* [for example, by attacking them], there is reason to suppose that the latter do not have the right to do *x*—certainly not a 'felicitous' [meaningful] right."[210]

The contractual retributive justification of transitional justice arises from a reluctance to accept difficult-to-prove metaphysical justifications of individual rights, relying instead on contractual social theories. Contractual social theory has a well known history and is doubtless quite familiar to the reader; Carlos Nino and others have adapted it to justifying criminal accountability in transitional nations.[211] Because contractual justifications of punishment depend to a certain extent on a criminal's awareness of his acts' criminality, these justifications tend to rely on international behavioral norms and law as a basis for prosecution.[212] 9

Of course, moral intuitionism is the most emotionally powerful justification for prosecuting and punishing wrongdoers. Human rights advocates in particular give victims' stories ample play in their writing. This appeal is the heart of Cassese's "forgetting makes a mockery of the dead."[213] And any blithe advocate of official forgiveness through amnesty would be admonished to remember one South African woman's testimony to the TRC:

> After learning for the first time how her husband had died, she was asked if she could forgive the man who did it. Speaking slowly, in one of the native languages, her message came back through the interpreters: "No government can forgive." Pause. "No commission can forgive." Pause. "Only I can forgive." Pause. "And I am not ready to forgive." [214]

These moral arguments become particularly relevant to the rhetoric of justice when prosecuting wrongdoers is politically difficult. Utilitarian arguments for justice have a way of being matched by utilitarian arguments against justice—namely that insisting on justice will slow a

---

9.   Carlos Nino writes, "Consent to criminal responsibility is implied when one acts voluntarily, with knowledge that punishment for that act is a necessary normative consequence of its performance. To assure the requisite knowledge, that normative consequence must be established by the laws in force when the act is committed." (*Radical Evil on Trial*, 148.)

transition from authoritarianism. Most international lawyers are willing to compromise, but speak of a moral duty to prosecute as a way of ensuring that an outgoing regime receives the harshest penalty feasible.

Before closing this discussion of the liberal-prosecutorial model of transitional justice, I should note that both utilitarian and moral reasons are used to argue for the application of liberal procedural standards in transitional justice. Mark Osiel's recent attempt to justify "liberal show trials" aside,[215] there remains a strong taboo against trials that do not provide defendants at least the minimum civil rights stipulated in international treaties. Trials that fail to guarantee defendants' rights risk being perceived as illegitimate, and political "victor's justice" is neither moral nor able to achieve justice's utilitarian ends. The specter of Stalin's show trials haunts discussions of transitional justice.

The Model's Failure in Rwanda

Both Rwanda's government and the international community initially pursued liberal-prosecutorial justice for the men and women responsible for the 1994 genocide. Killers were to be held accountable for their actions as a way of deterring future violence, promoting the rule of law, and creating a history of the genocide.[216]

Today, this model stands as a failure in Rwanda. The failure is twofold. First, the liberal prosecutorial model of justice has in Rwanda failed to deliver justice to those being prosecuted. Rwanda's courts remain overwhelmed. The 6,000 verdicts rendered since 1996 represent fewer than 5 percent of the 125,000 inmates languishing in prison on genocide charges. Prosecutors concede that 15 percent of those in jail may be innocent,[217] while the government admits that the courts will require over a century to clear the caseload.[218] The government has been forced to thrice extend the legal limit on pre-trial detentions in order to keep the inmates in jail.[219]

Prison conditions are squalid. Prisons are filled to several times their intended capacity, inmates are often forced to rely on their families for food, and thousands have died while awaiting their trials.[220] Given Rwanda's life expectancy (under 50 for men) and the pace of justice, Rwanda's genocide courts condemn most inmates to death in prison.

Despite the injustice of this situation, material constraints prevent the Rwandan government from improving it. The entire governmental budget for year 2002 is approximately USD $200,000,000,[221] and more than 15% percent already flows to prisons, courts, and reparations. Even if Rwanda could find the financial resources to establish additional genocide courts, shortages of trained personnel would probably prevent it from doing so. Yet the alternative of simply freeing the prisoners would abandon the pursuit of justice.

The ICTR, with its more lavish budget of USD $80,000,000[222] per year, has indicted a mere 61 suspects. Because it defines its mission as prosecuting top members of the Habyarimana government, it will never significantly reduce Rwanda's caseload.

The second failure of justice has been its inability to promote the utilitarian goals of liberal-prosecutorial transitional justice. Rwanda remains an authoritarian state. The rule of law has not been fully consolidated, as is evidenced by sporadic government harassment of political opponents.[223] Judging from prisoners' lack of remorse, justice has had an at-best tenuous deterrent effect. Finally, reconciliation and ethnic harmony is scarce. There are remarkable stories of individual reconciliation, but any protracted conversation with Rwandans reveals a nation that remains deeply divided.

In some respects, justice has even worsened the situation. Its' slow pace relative to the number of inmates has reduced the legitimacy of the current government. Many Hutu suspect that they are being imprisoned by a Tutsi government as revenge—not justice—and doubt that they will ever be released. The government's legitimacy has been further reduced by the paucity of trials for RPF-sponsored atrocities. Meanwhile, long lines make the burden of feeding an imprisoned family member onerous, and families are often sorely in need of the labor of the men behind bars.

The ICTR may be having a deterrent effect on human rights crimes in the international arena, though that is hard to measure. It does not, however, have any sort of impact in Rwanda. The distance between Arusha and Rwanda ensures that few Rwandans have ever seen the Tribunal, and low levels of television and radio penetration prevent Rwandans from learning of its work remotely. Rwandans who do express an opinion of the ICTR, mainly urban Tutsi, are wholly negative. They disagree with the international community's view that spending $80,000,000 a year to prosecute a handful of suspects is an efficacious allotment of scarce donor-nation resources. With some justification, they argue that the ICTR skims money away from desperately needed development projects. In the absence of popular knowledge of the ICTR—and given that those few Rwandans who do follow its work view the Tribunal as a folly—it is difficult to see how the Tribunal can have a positive impact on Rwanda.

Some of these failings are due to unanticipated logistical difficulties. Neither the RPF nor the international community had good estimates of the numbers of killers or victims in 1994, and neither adequately considered the genocide's impact on the state's capacity to deliver justice. From a material perspective, the liberal prosecutorial model of transitional justice is simply not viable in Rwanda.

The liberal-prosecutorial model of transitional justice more fundamentally fails Rwanda, however, because of the model's development in the context of crimes of states. Such crimes, I argued, are typically planned by small groups of elites, violate existing laws, and are committed in secret—consequently the purpose of justice is to eliminate such elites' potential to control a state.

Rwanda's genocide, however, is equally what Professor Alvarez terms "crimes of hate." This is violence that is "the product of homegrown struggles" within communities.[224] Crimes of hate are committed or at least tolerated by a high proportion of the population—the "culture of impunity" extends to the masses. Histories of Rwanda's

genocide, for example, are rife with horrific accounts of neighbors killing neighbors and even family members killing their kin.

Justice in the wake of crimes of hate must therefore accomplish different ends than justice following crimes of states. The two dominant
ends are moral re-education—teaching a complicitous population the
impermissibility of killing—and reconciliation. I will argue that these
goals are best accomplished by what I call the "communitarian restorative model of transitional justice."[10] But first we must examine exactly
what justice must accomplish in post-atrocity societies like Rwanda.

Communitarian restorative Transitional Justice

The great Romanian sociologist Emile Durkheim thought that societies punished wrongdoing to both express and preserve their shared
conception of morality.[225] Durkheimian punishment is a way of
"indicating that the sentiments of the collectivity have not changed,
that the communion of minds sharing the same beliefs remains absolute, and that, in this way, the injury that the crime has inflicted upon
society has been made good."[226] Punishment's primary effect is on
"honest people" by "forestalling in minds already distressed any fresh
weakening of the collective psyche."[227] It thereby serves to affirm
shared values and social cohesion.

"Crimes of hate" such as the Rwandan genocide challenge one of
Durkheim's presuppositions: that societies share a moral objection to
atrocity. Rwandans' complicity in murder is staggering. Perhaps
160,000 participated, and millions more saw but did nothing to stop
the killing.[11] This situation constitutes what Carlos Santiago Nino calls
"radical evil," "violence in situations where acting violent is simply not
deviant."[228] Today, one finds all too little remorse among those who

---

10. My thinking about communitarian restorative justice, and the notion that dif-
     ferent sorts of transitional societies have different needs, is heavily influenced by
     Mark Drumbl's "Punishment, Postgenocide."
11. For example, families who fed and cared for a husband or father they knew was
     engaged in the killing.

killed. The overwhelming majority of prisoners refuse to admit the wrongness of their actions.[229] The tragic truth of Rwanda's killing fields is that few Rwandans appear to possess a deep moral objection to the genocide. As journalist Philip Gourevitch writes in his superbly narrated account of 1994, "During the genocide, the work of the killers was not regarded as a crime in Rwanda; it was effectively the law of the land and every citizen was responsible for its administration.[230]

Justice in this context must re-educate society at large. Only by instilling a sense of the fundamental wrongness of killing can security be maintained over the long term.

Seeing justice as education has a certain moral foundation. Jean Hampton, a philosopher at the University of Arizona, argued in a 1984 *Philosophy and Public Affairs* article that punishment is a society's way of providing a wrongdoer with a moral education. Tongue in cheek, she begins by drawing an analogy between traditional deterrence theory and the electrified fences that shepherds use to keep their cattle from straying:

> Punishments are like electrified fences. At the very least they teach a person, via pain, that there is a "barrier" to the action she wants to do, and so, at the very least they aim to deter.[231]

She then draws a subtle distinction between this classical view and her theory. which holds that punishment seeks to deter crime, but to deter it in a particular manner. It does so by teaching offenders the immorality of their crime.

> [The] 'fences' are marking *moral* boundaries, [and] the pain which these 'fences' administer (or threaten to administer) conveys a larger message to beings who are able to reflect on the reasons for these barriers' existence: they convey that there is a barrier to these actions *because* they are morally wrong….[The] theory maintains that punishment is intended as a way of teaching the wrongdoer that the action she did (or wants to do) is forbidden because it is morally wrong and should not be done for that reason.[232]

This passage parallels thoughts that Robert Nozick developed in his 1981 book, *Philosophical Explanations*. After breaking the thought-process behind retributive theories of punishment into nine logical statements, Nozick argues that retributivists view punishment as a particular type of communication with a wrongdoer—one that conveys what H.P. Grice has termed a "nonnatural meaning." This is a meaning that requires the audience to understand both the communication and a particular intent behind that communication.

In his influential article "Meaning," Grice writes that the statement "A meant something by x" is equivalent to the statement "A uttered x with the intention of inducing a belief [in an audience] by means of the recognition of that intention."[233] By this definition, Nozickian retributive punishment fails if the convict learns only that certain actions bring certain punishments. The convict must understand why those actions bring the punishments they do.

Nozick posits that punishment communicates two nonnatural meanings. First, punishment sends the message "this is how wrong what you did was."[234] Second, punishment "effects a connection with correct values for those who have flouted them.[235] Even if wrongdoers refuse to accept the values of those responsible for punishment, they recognize that they are being punished because those values were flouted. And punishment's infliction of pain (or deprivation of liberty) ensures that correct values have a tangible impact on the wrongdoer's life regardless of his acceptance of them.[236] Judges telling recidivist convicts, or, for that matter, parents telling children, "you'll have time to reflect" while in prison (or a child's room) are evidence of the fact that punishment conveys a moral-laden message.[237]

Hampton's moral education theory hybridizes Nozick's view with traditional deterrence theory. "The ultimate goal of punishment," she writes, "is not merely to deter the child from performing the bad action in the future, but to deter her *by convincing her* (as well as other children) to renounce the action because it is wrong."[238]

Punishment need not educate only those being punished. Civil dis-
obedience provides a powerful demonstration of this. It relies on the
seemingly unjust punishment of a lawbreaker to alter people's perception of the *law's* morality.[239] Trials, too have an uncanny ability to
spark moral dialogue and to promote the reconsideration of previously
held beliefs. Executed correctly, trials have the potential to educate the
moral sense of those people watching them. In Rwanda, this education
must be a central goal of justice.

Justice in Rwanda must also promote reconciliation. Mark Drumbl
of the University of Arkansas recently identified Rwanda as a "dualist
postgenocidal society," one in which "both victim and aggressor must
live unavoidably side-by-side within the same nation-state, occupy the
same territory, and share common public spaces."[240] Rwandans' mass
complicity in the genocide and ethnically-mixed settlement patterns in
fact make it a paradigmatic example of such a society: victims live quite
literally next door to those who killed their families. They must share
water supplies, fields, stores, village commons, and schools.

Justice in dualist post-genocidal societies must address the issue of
reconciliation—both between victims and offenders and between
offenders and their communities.[241] It is simply implausible and arguably immoral to imprison indefinitely a significant fraction of a
nation's population. Prisoners' potential labor and the material drain
of imprisonment are simply too great. In Rwanda, even survivors are
recognizing this: one Tutsi woman told the author that the "strong
men" in the prisons needed to be out working the fields and rebuilding
the country. And even if all offenders are prosecuted and punished,
they will eventually be released and returned to their communities. Justice must prepare all parties—victims, communities, and wrongdoers—for the day that occurs.

I posit that a "communitarian restorative" model of transitional justice is needed to accomplish the educative and reconciliatory goals of
justice in Rwanda. The communitarian restorative model holds that

justice should be implemented in local communities by local communities, and that it should draw on restorative justice principles to promote reconciliation.[242] Instead of centralized state-administered courts meting out formal justice, less formal local committees must take control of justice, encourage broad participation in the process, promote reconciliation between victims and wrongdoers, and prepare communities to welcome back wrongdoers after they complete their punishment. Punishments should include community service, restitution, and shame—potent tools for moral re-education and reconciliation—as well as traditional penal confinement.

Communitarian restorative justice is community-based because community-based proceedings have the greatest educative impact. Part of this is logistical—in many of the nations most in need of moral education, the only way to see a trial is to attend it in person. This is certainly true in Rwanda, where the absence of modern mass communications technology[12] prevents Rwandans from experiencing justice they cannot walk to.

Legitimacy is the other reason that community based justice is more likely than state-administered justice to alter morality. Studies suggest that observers of judicial processes value the sense that "community members have been treated fairly by someone who understands their arguments."[243] The greater legitimacy of local forums is likely to be particularly pronounced in dualist-postgenocidal societies, which are frequently suspicious of the central government. Justice will not have an educative impact if it is seen as illegitimate.[244]

---

12.   Although Rwanda has developed a very modern digital cellular network in its cities, radio and television penetration in the countryside remain minimal. According to the *CIA World Factbook*, Rwanda had 600,000 radios and perhaps 1,000 televisions in 1997. The television figure has probably risen dramatically, but no more than a few thousand televisions sets serve a population of 8 million. Radios in Rwanda are shared—it is common to see groups of men standing in a circle and listening to a small portable radio—but music is far more popular than news.

This is a particularly germane concern in Rwanda given Hutu mistrust of the government-appointed judges serving on Rwanda's genocide courts. There is evidence that both prisoners and rural Hutu see Rwanda's existing genocide courts as imposing victors' justice.[245] Localizing justice should restore its legitimacy.

Reconciliation can be promoted by drawing on restorative justice theory. Restorative justice is predicated on the belief that crime "involves some domination of us that reduces our freedom to enjoy life as we choose."[246] Crime is first and foremost an attack on a particular victim and on a community, and only distantly an offense against the state.[247] The central goals of restorative justice, therefore, are to repair injuries and reconcile disputants, and to ensure the security of the community.[248] Restorative justice accomplishes these goals by restoring victims, strengthening communities, and morally educating wrongdoers through the use of shame.

"Disempowerment," writes the Australian criminologist John Braithwaite, "is part of the indignity of being a victim of crime."[249] Yet state-administered courts further compound victim disempowerment by placing justice in the hands of lawyers and impartial administrators with no personal stake in the crime.[250] Although this protects the defendants' rights—and differentiates justice from revenge—it frequently leaves both victims and communities feeling that justice has not been done.[251] Victims find it difficult to find a sense of closure or move on in their lives, much less reconcile themselves to their wrongdoers. Communities, meanwhile, frequently do not achieve a greater sense of security and wonder what will happen when the wrongdoer is released from prison.

The procedures vary, but restorative justice empowers communities by returning justice to their hands. Community members are expected to mediate a mutually acceptable solution to the dispute. At the proceedings, both the victim and the defendant have ample opportunity to speak on their own behalf and are encouraged to invite friends or colleagues to do so as well. This empowers the victim by assigning her a role in determining the appropriate penalty, which typically involves an apology and restitution of some sort.[252] The wrong, if not undone, is partially rectified. Defendants, on the other hand, have the opportunity to explain their motivations (desperation, etc.) so that the victim and community can get a clearer picture of their position.[253] Restorative justice posits that this sort of scenario is conducive to reconciling victims and defenders and facilitates their coexistence within a community.[254]

Restorative theory eschews adversarial procedures. The spirit of proceedings emphasizes all participants' right to speak their views without fear that their own reputations will be attacked on cross-examination. The point is to restore—not to win—and it is thought that adversarial proceedings merely encourage all parties to take hard-line positions and adopt a "bunker mentality."

The reconciliatory potential of restorative justice is also seen as a tool to strengthen civil society and to weave a strong social fabric of trust.[255] The collapse of America's inner cities during the 1970s and 1980s, a time when American courts incarcerated an ever-larger percentage of the inner-city population, demonstrates the failure of state-administered justice to develop civil society or even secure communities. Local forums of justice that bring together and empower otherwise atomic community members can assist in rebuilding local civil society. There is already some evidence that reintroduced "Village Courts" in Papua New Guinea are having this effect.[256]

Restorative justice challenges commonly-held notions that penal confinement is the most appropriate form of punishment. Shame and community service are used instead—the first to alter behavior, and the second to make wrongdoers rebuild some of what they destroyed. Penal confinement has a poor record of moral education. Instead of reducing deviance by exposing wrongdoers to acceptable norms of behavior, it amplifies deviance by restricting already-deviant individuals to a community of like-minded fellows.[257] The harshness of prison and modern justice's other punitive tools may prevent future crimes through deterrence, but most prisoners released after a period of peer-affirmation of deviance feel little remorse for past wrongs and lack moral compunction against future offenses—so long as the odds of getting caught seem low.

Braithwaite suggests that shaming is a superior approach to punishment that affords a real possibility of wrongdoers' moral education.[258] Shame punishes by playing on a wrongdoer's moral sentiments and, ideally, will fuel an internal desire for moral reform. Making a wrongdoer hear his victim's story—ideally in a context where the wrongdoer's action will be censured by those he loves and respects—can powerfully affect his conscience.

Of course, shame has a long history of use as a penal tool. Criminals once faced the pillory, the stocks, and worse.[259] These penal practices were discontinued because they came to be seen as both excessively harsh and ineffective: wrongdoers were so stigmatized that they became a "class of outcasts"[260] who frequently withdrew into communities of like-minded individuals who reinforced deviant tendencies.[261]

Braithwaite draws a distinction between this type of "disintegrative shaming" and his proposal of "reintegrative shaming" of wrongdoers. "Reintegrative shaming," he writes, "means that expressions of community disapproval…are followed by gestures of acceptance into the community of law-abiding citizens."[262] A community must demonstrate the wrongdoer that he will again be welcome in the community if he reforms his behavior. Otherwise he has little incentive to do so.

Shaming a wrongdoer will be most effective if done in the presence of individuals that the wrongdoer respects. Moral approbation or rebukes are most powerful when delivered by such individuals, not by anonymous strangers who can be dismissed and forgotten.[263] Restorative justice's success in modifying behavior therefore depends somewhat on assembling an appropriate group of people to participate in determining a wrongdoer's sentence and in shaming him. Family members are typically urged to attend restorative justice hearings, and the hearings are moderated by respected individuals within the community[264]—the weight of these individuals' presence is conducive to moral education. A wrongdoer who understands the wrongness of his acts and repents is unlikely to offend again.

Community service has several benefits as punishment. First and foremost, it requires wrongdoers to help rebuild the community damaged by their crime. It also encourages reconciliation by letting victims and community members see a productive product of the wrongdoers' labor. Finally, from the wrongdoer's perspective, community service can develop new, marketable skills.

Given Rwandans' high complicity and ethnically intermixed settlement patterns, communitarian restorative justice is required to promote moral reeducation and reconciliation nationally. Rwanda's existing courts have already demonstrated that liberal-prosecutorial justice does not promote reconciliation in dualist post-genocidal societies. The sorts of deliberative, local forums proposed by restorative theory, however, afford hope of achieving that goal.

At least in Rwanda, communitarian restorative justice will require the simplification of judicial procedure. Rwanda's educational system has left half the population illiterate and has ill-prepared many citizens to understand the complex procedures of liberal courts, let alone serve as judges in them.

Simplifying justice may further enhance its legitimacy. Western citizens tend to accept the legitimacy of judicial verdicts precisely because complex procedures are presumed to forestall miscarriages of justice, but in Rwanda such procedures may in fact delegitimize justice by making it incomprehensible to the citizenry it serves.

The greater legitimacy of local forums in Rwanda would be particularly conducive to reconciliation. Hutu have been reluctant to confess wrongdoing to the existing genocide courts because they distrust the courts' motives and impartiality.[265] Hutu would presumably be more willing to confess, and perhaps apologize, in front of a local panel they deemed trustworthy. These confessions, particularly in conjunction with restitution, would help to heal the relationship between victim and wrongdoer.[13]

The restorative idea of reintegrative shaming is useful in developing a form of justice that will promote moral education. Rwandan agnosticism on genocide's immorality would initially appear to militate against reintegrative shaming. It is, after all, unlikely that a man would be ashamed of his having committed a widely condoned act. If, however, the local forums responsible for justice are comprised of respected community members who oppose genocide, they may be able to instill in wrongdoers a sense of shame that wider Rwandan society cannot.

Shame alone seems a deeply insufficient penalty for genocide. It is certainly one that victims will view as insufficient; in Rwanda, reconciliation will require harsher punishments. Empowering local forums to determine those punishments, however, will enhance their legitimacy.

In summary, the communitarian restorative model of transitional justice envisions that justice will take place in, and be managed by, local communities. It will have simplified, deliberative procedures that give both victims and wrongdoers substantive roles in the justice process. The aims of communitarian restorative justice are to alter morality and to promote reconciliation.

Communitarian restorative justice is not appropriate for all transitional societies. But in dualist post-genocidal societies such as Rwanda, where tremendous numbers of people are complicit in genocide and poverty and destruction militate against the educative potential of any other system of justice, communitarian restorative justice affords the best chance of altering morality, ensuring security, and promoting reconciliation.

---

13. Restitution is a particularly important concept in Rwandan culture. Conversations with victims reveals that many desire contrition and reparations as much, if not more, than punitive justice.

Gacaca Justice

The Rwandan government proposed gacaca jurisdictions in 1999 as a way of speeding the pace of genocide trials.[266] The proposal was held to have two main virtues. Firstly, it would reduce the long-term cost of prisons and justice. Secondly, it would eliminate the injustice of prolonged detention without trial. This offers the added benefit of reducing international human rights organizations' complaints about Rwandan prisons, which put a black mark on Rwanda's applications for international aid.

Almost immediately, both the Rwandan government and international lawyers with an interest in restorative justice recognized the restorative potential of gacaca jurisdictions, which is, after all, patterned on traditional justice that emphasizes community decision-making, shame, reparations, and reintegration. By the time the Rwandan Parliament passed the gacaca law, its preamble was revised to include two statements that emphasize its restorative potential: "Considering the necessity, in order to achieve reconciliation and justice in Rwanda," and "Considering that it is important to provide for penalties allowing convicted prisoners to amend themselves and to favour their reintegration into the Rwandese society...."[267]

Indeed, gacaca appears to include most of the elements of the communitarian restorative model of justice. Having argued that Rwanda needs such a model, I now turn to gacaca to assess it in this light.

3

GACACA JUSTICE

Gacaca originally denoted a variety of grass common to Rwanda's hills. Long before the colonial period, the word came to refer to the system of justice that village elders dispensed while sitting on gacaca-covered ground.

Gacaca, like other systems of indigenous justice in Africa, does not appear to have had formal procedures, and there were probably significant regional variations.[268] In broad outline, village elders called *Inyangamugayo* convened all parties to a crime[1] and would work to mediate a solution that typically resulted in the wrongdoer giving reparations or making some other show of contrition. Gacaca sessions often ended with the two parties sharing a drink or meal as a demonstration of reconciliation.[269] Serious offenses, or cases where the elders deemed the offered reparations too low, could result in the wrongdoer being ostracized from the community or turned over to government chiefs for more severe punishment.[270]

Gacaca survived Europeans' arrival in Rwanda, though in 1924 the colonial administration limited the system's jurisdiction to civil and commercial matters and it slowly died out in the larger cities.[271] Much the same pattern prevailed in the post-colonial order, with village elders retaining authority to mediate small property disputes, marital tiffs, and the like.

In the countryside, gacaca re-emerged immediately after the 1994 genocide to provide a forum for dispute resolution during a period

---

1.   These could be individuals. However, Rwanda's strong family structure often meant that gacaca mediated disputes between extended families.

when the state had little capacity to administer justice.[272] In subsequent years, some village gacacas sought to promote accountability and reconciliation for crimes committed during the genocide.[273] The new RPF-dominated government encouraged this trend as a way of re-establishing order. In some cases it even took the initiative, for example by establishing gacaca councils in prisons to resolve prisoner disputes and to mediate relations between inmates and the genocide courts.[274]

The first discussions of using gacaca justice to try inmates for their crimes during the genocide occurred in 1995. However, international donors were skeptical, and human rights groups expressed concern that gacaca would fail to protect defendants' rights. Those concerns and, one suspects, RPF fears that gacaca would be lenient towards genocidaires, caused the government to reject the idea.

Despair over the ever-growing prison population and the slow pace of justice during the late 1990s brought the idea back under consideration in 1999.[275] The concerns about defendants' rights and leniency remained, but injustice and the costs of indefinite imprisonment made the proposal more attractive than it had been four years earlier. After clearing the idea with international donors, Rwanda's Parliament passed Organic Law 40/2000 on October 12, 2000 (hereafter referred to as the "gacaca law"). This law established nearly 11,000 "gacaca jurisdictions" and empowered them to try all but the most serious genocidaires, beginning late 2002.

There are significant differences between the modernized "gacaca jurisdictions" and traditional gacaca, not the least of which is that positive law established the gacaca jurisdictions. The jurisdictions are more formally constituted, have regularized procedures, and seek to protect defendants' rights in ways alien to the traditional variety. The remainder of this chapter is dedicated to describing the gacaca jurisdictions' operation.

Structure and Work of the Gacacas:[2],[3]

Rwanda's original 1996 Genocide Law divided genocide suspects into 4 categories. They are as follows:[276]

> Category 1: Suspects "whose criminal acts or whose acts of criminal participation place them among the planners, organizers, instigators, supervisors and leaders of the crime of Genocide or of a crime against humanity." This includes people who held positions of authority in government, the army, religious organizations and militias; "notorious murderers" who exhibited "zeal or excessive malice" in the commission of crimes; and people suspected of committing rape or sexual torture.

> Category 2: Suspects who participated in physical assaults that resulted in the death of the victim.

> Category 3: Suspects accused of serious assaults that did not result in death.

> Category 4: Suspects accused of looting, theft, or other property crimes.

The gacacas have jurisdiction over suspects in categories 2 through 4. Category 1 suspects, who face the death penalty, will remain under the jurisdiction of Rwanda's genocide courts.

The gacaca jurisdictions are divided into four categories, each of which corresponds to an administrative level of Rwandan local government. The cell is the lowest administrative level, consisting of 10

---

2. For the remainder of this thesis, I use "gacaca," "gacacas" and "gacaca jurisdictions" interchangeably to refer to the gacaca jurisdictions. "Traditional gacaca" will be called by that name.

3. All information about the gacacas, unless otherwise noted, is taken directly from the gacaca law or from the *Manuel Explicatif* that will be used to train judges. This was prepared by the Rwandan Supreme Court and Lawyers Without Borders. At the end of each sub-section I have included a footnote with a reference to the relevant document.

extended family groupings and usually numbering several hundred individuals. There are approximately 9,500 cells nationwide. Above the cells are 1,550 sector administrations, which are themselves grouped into 106 districts. Twelve Prefectures, and a special administrative district for the city of Kigali, comprise the top level of Rwandan local government and roughly correspond to American states.[277] Each gacaca is empowered to hear crimes stemming from the genocide within its territorial jurisdiction, while temporal jurisdiction extends for acts committed between October 1, 1990 to December 31, 1994.

Although all 11,000 gacacas will contribute to investigating and trying genocide suspects, they are not all charged with the same tasks. Cell-level gacacas will begin the gacacas's work by investigating and making a record of the genocide within the cell. They will compile a list of those injured and killed by the genocide, record the crimes committed against each individual on the list, and identify the suspect or suspects accused of each crime. The purpose of this investigation is twofold. Primarily, it is to identify genocide suspects so that they can later be prosecuted and tried. However, the Rwandan government also sees this procedure as a way of creating the documentary basis for a future comprehensive history of the genocide.

Cell-level gacacas will then use this information to sort the suspects into one of the four categories. It is expected that the majority of suspects, perhaps as high as 80 percent, will fall into Category 2.[278]

Trials will begin following this categorization process, most likely 6 months to a year after the cell-level gacacas begin their work.[279] Different level gacacas are responsible for hearing the cases of different categories of suspects. Cell-level gacacas will try Category 4 suspects, sector level gacacas will try category 3 suspects, and district level-gacacas will try Category 2 suspects and hear any appeals of sector-level gacacas' decisions. Prefecture-level gacacas exist solely to hear the appeals of Category 2 suspects, who cannot then appeal to the regular courts.[280]

Each gacaca jurisdiction is comprised of a General Assembly, a Seat, a Coordinating Committee, and a President. The General Assembly of cell-level gacacas is comprised of every adult (18 years or older) cell resident. Last October, the cell-level gacacas' General Assemblies each elected five representatives to serve on the General Assembly of a sector-level gacaca, which in turn elected representatives to serve on the district and prefecture-level gacacas.

At all gacaca levels, each gacaca General Assembly chose 19 of its members to serve as the gacaca's Seat. These Seat members are the gacaca's judges. Each Seat in turn elected a President, two Secretaries and two Vice Presidents, who together comprise the gacaca's Coordinating Committee. These individuals are required to be literate in Kinyarwanda, while the President and Secretaries must additionally have completed at least 6 years of primary education.[281]

The large number of judges per gacaca means that some 260,000 Rwandans—about 6 percent of the country's adult population—are serving. This perhaps the largest experiment in popular justice in modern history.

Once the process beings, the gacacas will hold a variety of different sorts of hearings. The Seat of a gacaca is to meet regularly in public to fill out forms, determine its schedule, and generally ensure the smooth functioning of the gacaca. It can also meet witnesses privately in order to encourage testimony—though if the gacaca is actively trying a case, the defendant has the right to be present at all hearings where testimony is given against him.

At least initially, cell-level gacacas will collect most of their evidence during General Assembly meetings, which may occur as frequently as once a week. The gacaca's President presides over these meetings. He is responsible for setting the agenda, maintaining order, encouraging testimony, recognizing speakers, and otherwise managing the meeting's flow. Members of a cell-level gacaca's General Assembly (all adults) are expected to attend regularly, in order to be present if called upon to testify.[282]

At the cell level, most hearings will be held outdoors—perhaps sitting on the very grass that gives the process its name. The President begins a session of the gacaca by calling the Seat and audience to order and announcing the day's business. If the gacaca is collecting evidence to record the genocide in the cell, the President solicits general contributions from the audience. He asks for the names of those killed or injured, the type of injury, and identities of any suspects. The state prosecutor's office is welcome to contribute any information that it has collected. The President is to maintain order and create an atmosphere conducive to testifying, being particularly aware that many victims remain scared and reluctant to speak.

Once a cell-level gacaca's Seat has identified the genocide victims within its jurisdiction and created a list of suspects, it turns to collecting the evidence needed to categorize the latter. At public hearings (not necessarily General Assembly meetings) the Seat can take testimony about particular suspects, ask the state prosecutor for evidence, and make decisions to search property. After collecting evidence, the Seat can retire *in camera* to assign suspects' categories. The suspect cannot appeal his categorization.

Gacacas will begin to judge the accused after all suspects have been categorized nationwide.[283] Suspects' names and files pertaining to them are transferred to the relevant gacaca: district, sector or cell. Hearings will take place in public, and schedules are to published in advance so that witnesses have the opportunity to attend. Those who refuse to testify, or who lie to the gacaca, risk a 1 to 3 year prison sentence.

A gacaca's President presides over its trial hearings. One of the gacaca's Secretaries is to take note of each day's proceedings. All 19 members of the gacaca Seat act as a jury, following the proceedings and ultimately determining a suspect's guilt.

The President begins by announcing each case and introducing the suspect to the audience, stating his name, residence and the accusations against him. If the suspect wishes to confess his crimes, the president asks him to recount publicly all relevant details. The President then asks the assembled audience to reflect on the suspect's confession and testify as to its veracity. The suspect is allowed to modify his confession if he appears honestly to have forgotten some detail. The suspect must apologize as part of the confession process. The Seat then retires *in camera* and deliberates on whether the confession is full and complete. If it decides affirmatively, it can grant the defendant a reduced penalty.

If the suspect pleads his innocence, the President asks those in attendance—and the state prosecutor—to testify either for or against the suspect. If essential witnesses are absent, the case is to be postponed and the witnesses compelled to attend. As with other hearings, the President is to keep order to promote an atmosphere conducive to testimony. In particular, he is to encourage testimony by victims and others, such as women, who might ordinarily be reluctant to speak out. The hearing is to be run in a non-adversarial, deliberative manner, and lawyers are prohibited from taking any part in the proceedings. Both the defendant and victims are to be given opportunities to question any testimony that is contrary to their memory of events. The Seat can go *in camera* to take testimony if a witness fears that testifying in public would risk her safety or expose her to loss of face (e.g., testimony about rape), but the defendant has a right to be present and respond to any accusations. If no one comes forward to testify against the suspect and the public prosecutor can offer no evidence, the suspect is found not guilty by default and freed immediately.

After the public hearing, the Seat of the gacaca retires *in camera* to determine the suspect's guilt. Rwanda does not have a tradition of a presumption of innocence. During judicial training, however, the gacaca judges will be admonished to question testimony and to always be willing to doubt the suspect's guilt. The determination of guilt and penalty—like all of a gacaca Seat's decisions—is to be made by consensus. Failing that, a simple majority of the 19 will suffice.

Individuals serving on the gacaca's Seat are expected to recuse themselves from any decisions involving close friends or family members to the 2nd degree of kinship. Victims, defendants, and witnesses all have the right to request that a judge recuse herself. If she refuses, the Seat can deicide to exclude her from the decision.[284]

Category 2 and 3 defendants are entitled to appeal both verdicts and confessions denied by the gacaca that originally heard them. A defendant can appeal by stating his intention immediately after a verdict is announced, completing an appeal form, or, in the absence of forms, writing his appeal on a piece of paper and sending it to the relevant appellate gacaca. Defendants who do not immediately appeal their verdicts are given 15 days to file. The appellate gacaca is entitled to rehear the case *de novo*.[285]

The Rwandan government has established a new 6th Chamber within the Supreme Court to administer and oversee gacaca's administration. Its roles are myriad: it is responsible for training judges, coordinating the circulation of documents between gacacas, providing transportation for key witnesses otherwise unable to attend a hearing, coordinating the movement of defendants within the prisons, and training a pool of professional advisors able to answer any questions that a gacaca may have about the law or procedure.[286] The state prosecutors will also make a significant contribution. They are to continue investigating crimes committed during the genocide, and will pass any evidence they uncover against a suspect along to the relevant gacaca.

Punishment for Genocide

Rwanda's original 1996 genocide law provided substantially reduced penalties for suspects who confessed their crimes fully and apologized publicly. At the time, the government viewed this as both beneficial and necessary: it was supposed to speed the release of inmates who recognized the wrongness of their actions while promoting reconciliation by encouraging confession. This plea-bargaining arrangement has been carried over to the gacaca law.

Prior to the government's establishment of gacaca, relatively few suspects chose to avail themselves of the confession procedure. This was largely due to prisoners' suspicions of governmental intent. Many did not believe that confessing would actually result in more lenient treatment. It also appears that some inmates, fearing the revelation of their own crimes, threatened others in order to deter confession. Government mismanagement did little to assuage their fears. Suspects who confessed early in the process frequently found that overtaxed local prosecutors were simply unable to verify the confession or complete the paperwork necessary for release. The detainees' continued detention confirmed fears of governmental insincerity.[287]

The announcement of gacaca greatly expanded the number of suspected willing to confess—approximately a third have already prepared their confessions so as to be ready when gacaca starts. It is thought that a significant majority will eventually avail themselves of the confession procedure.[288]

The benefits of confessing depend on when a suspect confesses. An individual receives a greater reduction in his sentence if he chooses to confess prior to being named as a suspect. Once named, a suspect receives a smaller reduction so long as he confesses prior to the start of his gacaca trial.

With this in mind, sentencing guidelines are as follows:

Category 4 offenders must pay a civil penalty to compensate victims for stolen or destroyed property.

Category 3 offenders will receive between 1 and 3 years in prison if they confess prior to being named as suspects; 3 to 5 years of they confess prior to their trial, and 5 to 7 years if convicted or if their confession is rejected.

Category 2 offenders will receive between 7 and 12 years in prison if they confess prior to being named as suspects; 12 to 15 years if they confess prior to their trial, and 25 years to life if convicted or if their confession is rejected. In addition, those guilty of Category 2 offenses forfeit numerous civil rights: the right to vote, to carry a weapon or serve in the armed forces, to witness civil documents, to hold certain professional certifications, or to testify under oath. The government intends to develop a process by which offenders can petition for the restoration of their rights after an appropriate period of time.

Category 1 offenders, who are not tried by the gacacas, are only eligible for a penalty reduction if they confess prior to being named as suspects. They will be sentenced to a minimum of 25 years in prison, and those who do not confess face a capital penalty.

All of those convicted are to be given credit for time served.

The law stipulates a number of exceptions. Possession of a government office at the time of offense is an aggravating circumstance that earns the maximum permitted penalty. Category 1 suspects who were between 14 and 18 years old at the time of their crime will receive reduced sentences of 10 to 20 years in prison, though Category 2 and 3 suspects in this age group will be tried as adults. Those who were under 14 during the genocide will not be held criminally liable for their actions, but they will be sent to state reeducation centers.[289]

Category 2 and 3 suspects who take advantage of the confession process are eligible to have the second half of their sentence commuted to community service. Those who choose to participate in the community service scheme will be released from prison and free to return home, but are required to work three days a week on the community project to which they are assigned.

The Rwandan government is working with the NGO Penal Reform International to develop community service programs similar to those that the organization has established in Zimbabwe and elsewhere. The details remain to be determined, but convicts participating in community service will likely help build village schools and health clinics, maintain public spaces, and work on infrastructure projects. Local governments may administer some of the projects, but many convicts will be assigned to projects run by local NGOs. Those organizations will take responsibility for tracking attendance and reporting those who fail to fulfill their duties. Convicts deemed derelict will be remanded to prison.

Gacaca traditionally forced wrongdoers to pay restitution as a part of their punishment. Restitution's popularity endures today: 86 percent of Rwandans favor compensating the families of genocide victims.[290] Victims in particular support the idea, arguing that they personally need assistance in rebuilding shattered lives.

The gacaca law includes provisions for restitution. First, victims can request that damages be entered into the judgment against a guilty defendant and can seek civil penalties from them. Given the country's poverty, however, few offenders will be able to give more than token restitution.

Secondly, the state has taken it upon itself to provide some compensation. Gacacas are to forward copies of their judgments to the Compensation Fund for Victims of the Genocide and Crimes Against Humanity, which was established in 1999 and is funded by a 5 percent dedication of government revenue. The Compensation Fund will award damages to victims through a yet-to-be-determined formula that will likely include educational scholarships, superior medical care, and other services as well as direct compensation.[291]

Gacaca Judges

Rwanda elected the gacaca judges in October of 2001, in elections that were widely seen as free and fair.[292] Campaigning by victims' rights organizations, women's groups, and local NGOs seems to have ensured that both women and Tutsi are well represented on the gacacas. In the absence of statistical studies, anecdotal evidence indicates that a third of gacaca judges might be female while Tutsi make up 20 percent: overrepresented but not dramatically so.[293]

The gacaca law, in keeping with traditional gacaca, instructed Rwandans to select *Inyangamugayo* as judges. Traditionally, this term meant "village elder," but is today more broadly construed to be a respected and upright member of the community. The criteria specified in the law are as follows:[294]

1. Rwandan nationals.

2. 21 years old or older.

3. No criminal convictions resulting in a 6-month prison sentence (or greater) within the previous 5 years.

4. Cannot be genocide suspects.

5. Must have a local reputation for honesty, good behavior, and morals.

6. Must be free from "the spirit of sectarianism and discrimination."

7. Must be trustworthy.

8. Should be "characterized by a spirit of sharing speech;" i.e, should be comfortable speaking under pressure and in public places.

Members of certain professions are barred from serving on gacaca Seats or from being elected to the General Assemblies of higher-level gacacas. These include government employees, elected officials, police, soldiers, judges, clergy, and NGO employees.[295] Although these restrictions do limit the number of highly educated individuals serving as judges, they have the benefit of eliminating any appearance of governmental control of what is supposed to be a popular process.

No survey has yet been conducted of the judges to determine what sorts of people were elected. Anecdotal evidence, however, indicates that professionals, craftsmen, and traders are likely also overrepresented. The prevailing impression is that most are prosperous, settled, and middle-aged to old by Rwandan standards.[296]

District and prefecture-level gacaca judges appear to have on average better educations than their colleagues serving on lower-level gacacas, a result of the indirect elections for high-level gacaca judges. As a consequence, the best-qualified judges will hear the cases of suspects accused of the most serious crimes.

The gacaca judges will receive 6 days of formal training: 2 days per week for 3 weeks. Literate judges will also receive a detailed explanatory manual, while illiterate ones are to be given a pictographic guide and will be urged to consult others with questions about the process.[297]

The training focuses on both legal principles and gacaca's procedure. Judges will be taught to complete the necessary forms, manage the confession process, determine appropriate penalties, organize the public sessions, maintain order, and encourage testimony, etc. More broadly, they will be taught how to listen skeptically, what to consider when determining guilt and punishment, and other broad concepts.[298]

The adequacy of this training remains unclear. Many judges likely lack even basic education, and those who have attended school in the past may quite literally have not seen a printed word in years.[299] One woman involved in the training of judges reported that based on field tests, trainers could expect problems with attendance and even basic comprehension.

There are two reasons for hope that the education will be sufficient. Most of the difficult-to-learn tasks such as filling out forms are the responsibility of the President and Secretaries, who are required to have a basic education. The government, as mentioned earlier, is also training a pool of advisors to answer any questions that arise. Furthermore, judges on the higher-level courts are more likely to comprehend gacaca in a relatively short period of time for the reasons mentioned above.

Duration and Cost of Gacaca

The government estimates that gacaca will take 3 to 5 years once judges' training is complete. Less partial observers suspect that estimate is overly optimistic. Categorizing the suspects alone may take up to a year.[300] I expect that the trials will then take at least 5 years.

The predominance of Category 2 suspects is likely to limit the pace of the gacaca process. If 80 percent of the estimated 160,000 suspects do fall into Category 2, 108 district level gacacas will be responsible for 130,000 cases. Anecdotal evidence from government experiments with gacaca indicate a gacaca could hear several dozen confessions in a day, but that contested trials may take two or three days to complete. Even if most suspects confess, the district level gacacas will probably require 5–7 years to complete their work.[4]

Gacaca is not cheap. The official government contribution is expected to be 6 billion Rwandan francs (USD $13 million) over the course of the gacaca process, with just shy of 2 billion francs allocated in the 2002 budget.[301] The 6th Chamber of the Supreme Court is hoping that international donors will contribute material (cars, desks, etc.) and financial support that might double that figure.[302] Potential savings come primarily by reducing the expense of Rwanda's prisons, which currently cost the government more than USD $20 million per year.[303]

Preparing the Public for Gacaca:

Popular participation is crucial to the gacaca jurisdictions' success. Surveys show overwhelming popular support for the gacacas and indicate that that 87 percent of community members will be willing to testify.[304] Victim support, initially weak, has grown, while prisoners have been supportive since the beginning. Maintaining this support through the completion of the process is crucial to gacaca's success.

Government programs seek to educate the public about gacaca through both radio broadcasts and local forums. The radio campaign is designed around relatively long (minute plus) skits that highlight various aspects of gacaca,[305] while the forums rely on local government officials and NGO employees to educate small groups of community leaders. They, in turn, are expected to discuss gacaca with their neighbors.[306]

NGOs are also mounting their own, independent publicity efforts. Ibuka, the principal victims' rights organization, came out in favor of gacaca and is using its local representatives and newsletter to urge that survivors turn out to testify and otherwise participate in the process.[307] Other human rights groups have announced initiatives that

---

4.   Estimates are that about 80% of those in prison are guilty. If we extrapolate that figure out to include suspects who remain free, we can conjecture that 105,000 of 130,000 Category 2 suspects are guilty. Given the incentives for confessing, and the fact that other guilty pleas increase the likelihood that any individual suspect will be named as a perpetrator and will be convicted if tried, it seems plausible that 90% of guilty suspects will confess their crimes. On the basis of these figures, we can very roughly estimate the distribution of Category 2 cases as follows:

    Total Suspects: 130,000
    Total Guilty: 105,000
    Total Confessions: 95,000
    Total Not Guilty Pleas by Guilty Individuals: 10,000
    Total Not Guilty Pleas by Not Guilty Individuals: 25,000

    Assuming that a gacaca could hear 20 confessions or 1 to 2 trials each day, we can calculate that the District gacacas will require a total of about 4,800 days to hear confessions and 18,000-30,000 or so days to try suspects. 108 gacacas meeting 52 times a year could clear this caseload in 4 to 7 years. Including the time that the cell-level gacacas will take to collect evidence and categorize suspects, this figure implies that the gacaca process as a whole will take 5 to 8 years.

range from seminars for community opinion leaders to the distribution of newsletters in urban areas.

Closing Thoughts

In the previous chapter, I argued that Rwanda needed justice patterned on the communitarian restorative model. The gacaca jurisdictions were not developed with this intent—they were originally seen as a way of reducing justice's cost and the growing embarrassment of the seemingly indefinite detentions. However, there are clear parallels between gacaca and the communitarian restorative model I developed in the previous chapter. The next chapter seeks to assess gacaca's potential to achieve the communitarian restorative goals of moral education and reconciliation.

4

GACACA AS COMMUNITARIAN RESTORATIVE JUSTICE

Imagine this. Vianney is a man of 28 who has languished in a Rwandan prison since a neighbor accused him of participating in the genocide in late 1994. He has been reluctant to confess that he helped kill a neighbor—as a Hutu, he has a visceral mistrust of the RPF-dominated government—but he does feel some regret for what he did.

Vianney is summoned to appear before his district's gacaca jurisdiction, and on the appointed date finds himself standing in the central square of a town not far from his home. He studies the faces of the gacaca judges, measuring their temperaments, and realizes that one of them is a respected elder from his village. He notices that members of his family, as well as those of his victim, have turned out to witness the occasion. He sees the anguish in all their faces, and finds his heart flooded with guilt, shame, and remorse for his actions nearly a decade ago. Turning back to the judges, he realizes that his case has been called. He steps forward and, before his introduction is finished, announces that he would like to confess his crime and apologize publicly to his victim's family.

The President of the gacaca pauses, asks if he is certain, and then listens quietly as Vianney recounts his story. He had been conscripted into a band of killers led by a now-deposed local government official. He describes how they murdered their victim, and even admits to a related theft for which he had not been charged. The President asks those in attendance if the confession was complete, and two eyewitnesses attest to its veracity. Turning to Vianney, the President explains how the confession will be recorded and asks for an apology. Vianney hesitates, faces his victim's parents and young widow, and expresses his shame and remorse. He begs their forgiveness and vows that he will never again be the cause of such pain. They listen coldly, rage and sadness intertwined in their faces, and leave Vianney's appeal unanswered. But those nearby can sense a subtle shift in their demeanor, the beginnings of an acceptance of the sincerity of Vianney's apology. The gacaca accepts the confession and sentences Vianney to 13 years. With credit for time served he is eligible for release into the local community service program after the few weeks necessary to complete paperwork and finalize his placement.

Two months later the victim's widow comes to pay a visit. She has been reflecting on his apology, she says, and while she cannot find it in her heart to forgive, she states that she appreciated his sincerity and respects his recent work in rebuilding the local school. They both know that the tension between them will never fully fade, but accept that they must coexist within their community.

If repeated across Rwanda a hundred thousand times, this scenario is the ideal of gacaca. It is also, I think, a vision of communitarian restorative justice. It is certainly what Rwanda needs.

In chapter two, I argued that post-atrocity societies like Rwanda—characterized by intermixed settlement patterns, widespread complicity in wrongdoing, and deep poverty—needed to achieve security through moral reeducation and reconciliation within communities inhabited by both wrongdoers and victims. I maintained that the communitarian restorative model of transitional justice afforded the best opportunity of achieving these goals. In this chapter, I will assess gacaca's ability to accomplish these communitarian restorative goals. I begin by drawing out the parallels between gacaca and my model. I then discuss some of the problems that may arise and the government's plans to mitigate them. I will end on a positive note, because during my research in Rwanda I found several reasons for hope in the gacaca process' eventual success.

Gacaca as Communitarian restorative Justice

There are clear parallels between the Rwanda's plan for gacaca and my proposed communitarian restorative model of justice. Gacaca and communitarian restorative justice both emphasize local forums, popular participation, deliberative rather than adversarial procedures, and penalties that have a restitutional component.

Gacaca's locality bodes well for its ability to promote moral reform in Rwanda. Almost all Rwandans will participate in at least the cell gacacas' work: documenting the genocide within the cell, identifying suspects, and then categorizing them. Victims will have the opportunity to tell their stories, and of their suffering. This testimony will remind Rwandans who may be inclined to bury the past or see the genocide as a natural effect of civil war precisely how horrific it was. It will also educate the 50 percent of Rwandans who were under the age of 10 in 1994 about the genocide. Gacacas' role in educating younger Rwandans is particularly important in a nation whose schools have ceased to teach history.[1]

The stature of gacaca judges should facilitate gacaca's ability to turn this educative effect into moral reform. The low legitimacy of the existing genocide courts (and low popular knowledge of the ICTR) has severely limited their power to accomplish this goal. Suspects and their supporters, and others disinclined to condemn the genocide, can simply dismiss a guilty verdict as victors' justice and can disregard any potential moral lessons that come from seeing justice done. Communities themselves, on the other hand, have elected the gacaca judges.

---

1.   In Rwanda's charged atmosphere, choosing a curriculum has proven too controversial. (Interview with Klass De Jonge).

Their decisions will likely be accorded greater legitimacy and will carry a correspondingly greater moral weight. Seeing the respected senior members of Rwandan communities condemn someone for killing cannot be so easily dismissed and may encourage Rwandans to reassess their own views of the genocide's morality. Rwandans' natural tendency to turn to such individuals for advice should strengthen this effect.[308] Local condemnation should also make wrongdoers feel ashamed of their actions in a way they would not when facing a court they regard as illegitimate.

The moral educative effect may be particularly pronounced in younger Rwandans whose only real concept of the genocide derives from stories they have heard—which may not always be critical of genocidal killing. Developing an anti-genocidal morality in future generations is crucial to long-term stability.

Even if gacaca fails to develop a moral consensus against the 1994 genocide, it will familiarize Rwandans with peaceful forms of dispute resolution. The deliberative and consensus-based nature of gacaca decision-making will promote deliberation as a legitimate form of dispute resolution and may delegitimize future violence.

Gacaca also has a greater potential to promote reconciliation than do Rwanda's existing genocide courts. In line with restorative justice principles, it brings together victims and wrongdoers and allows each to tell his story in a deliberative, non-adversarial format. This promotes mutual understanding of others' positions, which is a crucial first step to reconciliation. For offenders, hearing victims' side of the story creates a feeling of remorse, while victims may find they have at least a modicum of sympathy for those offenders drafted into the killing. Adversarial procedures, on the other hand, encourage the adoption of hard-line attitudes and a "bunker mentality" that makes parties reluctant to reconcile even after a decision has been made resolving a dispute in favor of one side.

Gacaca's requirement that offenders apologize publicly as a precondition for their confessions' acceptance may further facilitate reconciliation. As with any situation where material benefits flow from an apology, not all apologies will be sincere. Some, however, will surely be backed by real remorse. Those will promote both the victim's sense of security, by assuring him that his attacker will not strike again, and a reconciliation between the two.

In a similar vein, gacaca's provisions for reparations should promote reconciliation. Even if reparations do not come directly from a wrongdoer—many are too poor to pay—the linking of nationally funded reparations with justice will provide additional solace to victims who are often still struggling to rebuild their lives and property. The gacacas' role in reparations should also strengthen their legitimacy in victims' eyes. This will reassure victims that the gacacas are doing justice.

The government's decision to allow offenders the option of serving half their sentence performing community service was almost certainly an economic one: convicts living at home and working on NGO-managed projects are not a burden to the state treasury.[309] Community service also has the additional potential to reconcile a wrongdoer with the larger community. It lets communities benefit from a wrongdoer's constructive work, rather than costing the community the expense of imprisoning him.[310] Rwandan communities desperately need the schools, heath centers, and other projects that have been proposed as community service projects. Seeing the "strong men" currently in prison out working to rebuild the country they tried to destroy should certainly have a reconciliatory effect on communities.

The community service program, taken together with the sentencing guidelines and the fact that prisoners will receive credit for time served, leads to an interesting conclusion. Category 2 prisoners arrested shortly after the genocide can confess and will be almost immediately eligible for release into a community service project. Category 3 prisoners will likely find their sentence complete by the time it is rendered.

Given the government's eagerness to reduce prison costs, this situation was likely seen as a benefit. From the victims' perspective, however, one has to ask: is this merely an amnesty in disguise?

There are four reasons for answering this question in the negative. Firstly, community service is still punishment. It is not as harsh as prison, but convicts still must give three days out of each week to their program. Failure to do so results in re-confinement. Secondly, not all prisoners will be released immediately. Those who were arrested in later years, or who do not confess early in the process will be detained for some years to come. Thirdly, gacaca may result in the imprisonment of a large number of killers (though smaller than the number now in jail) who are currently free. Finally, an amnesty would undermine all the benefits of the process of justice. Even if prisoners had served time prior to the amnesty, they would not have done so *because* they were being held accountable for any particular act. There would be no distinguishing between wrongdoers and the innocent, and hence no possibility of moral education. Reconciliation, too, would be difficult if victims were left without the solace that their victimizer's acts have been morally and legally condemned by a legitimate court.

Concerns

Gacaca's ability to promote reconciliation and moral change is dependent on its being accepted as justice. If people see gacaca as illegitimate or dysfunctional, they will have little inclination to participate in the process. This would both prevent the gacacas from achieving the goals of communitarian restorative justice and, given their dependence on popular participation, undermine their ability to try genocide suspects.

Conversely, popular support for gacaca will facilitate its success. The initial indicators are encouraging: 58 percent of respondents to a poll about gacaca were "highly confident that the jurisdictions will succeed in resolving the problems of trial of suspects" while another 29 percent were "fairly confident."[311] Initially hesitant about the process, victims are coming around and Ibuka's efforts to encourage victim participation will likely bolster their involvement. Journalists, meanwhile, report anecdotally that gacaca is popular with prisoners.[312] This comes as little surprise given their alternative is continued pre-trial detention.

There are, however, numerous concerns about gacaca. The system's very strengths—popular participation, community-selected judges, etc.—could fast become liabilities. Judges may prove biased, incompetent, or simply inconsistent. Alison Des Forges commented in a recent *New York Times* article, "[Rwandans] have selected 260,000 judges, most of whom have no training, no education beyond primary school."[313] If validated, any one of these concerns about judging could fundamentally undermine the gacacas' legitimacy and any hope for healing.

The Rwandan government has responded to concerns over the gacaca judges with safeguards intended to compensate for their lack of education and potential bias. As has already been mentioned, judges are expected to recuse themselves from cases involving close friends or family. Furthermore, the Seat of a gacaca jurisdiction is empowered to replace a judge who consistently exhibits a "culture of divisionism" or who "[fulfills] any act incompatible with the quality of an honest person."[314]

The government has also taken steps to compensate for the judges' poor education and the short training period allotted. As was mentioned earlier, senior members of gacacas' Coordinating Committees must be literate, and the 6th Chamber of the Supreme Court is training legal advisors whom judges can call upon with questions. The judicial training programs will emphasize that judges who feel they do not understand some aspect of the procedure can ask either other judges or these legal advisors.[315]

The indirect election of the senior gacaca judges is an additional safeguard against the incompetence and bias of the judges trying more severe crimes. Judges serving on higher-level gacacas will be drawn from a significantly wider geographic territory, resulting in a much lower chance that more than one or two of a gacaca's judges (if any) are familiar with any given defendant. Furthermore, they are expected to be on average better educated and better qualified for their positions.

A final safeguard comes from the defendants' right of appeal, and the appellate courts' power to hear cases *de novo*. Appellate jurisdictions can both remedy individual injustices and provide preemptive pressure against the bias of lower courts through the threat of overturning their decisions.

A separate set of concerns centers on the completeness and accuracy of testimony. One reporter covering gacaca test-runs in 2001 found witnesses more inclined to testify for defendants than against them.[316] This is likely due in part to rumors of defendants' intimidation of witnesses, compounded by the prospect of early release into a community service program.[317] Furthermore, the migration of people since the genocide inhibits the ability of some witnesses to return and testify near their former places of residence.[318]

As mentioned, however, the gacacas can promote full and accurate testimony in several ways.[319] The President is to maintain order and to encourage reluctant witnesses to speak out. Witnesses can also give testimony *in camera*. Finally, the gacacas are allowed to sentence witnesses who refuse to testify or who are deemed to be giving false testimony to a prison term of 1 to 3 years.

The Rwandan government is also taking national-level steps to promote testimony. Its gacaca publicity campaign is urging people to testify and warning of the consequences of refusing to do so.[320] The 6th Chamber of the Supreme Court has applied for international donations of vehicles and financial support for the transportation of witnesses.[321] Private organizations like Ibuka will parallel these government efforts with initiatives of their own.[322]

There is a bit of concern that gacacas will undermine reconciliation by prosecuting only Hutu crimes while ignoring RPF massacres. The gacaca law does not differentiate between RPF suspects and others, but the prosecutors' offices and central government administration have steadfastly denied systematic RPF human-rights abuses and have not investigated many allegations of them. The temporal and territorial jurisdiction of the law is a further built-in bias against trying RPF crimes. Many of those took place in 1996 in the Congo, when the RPF and RPF-backed militias killed at least tens of thousands and perhaps as many as 200,000 Hutu refugees.[323] Communities cannot very well be healed if one side senses that its grievances remain unanswered.

On the other hand, the gacacas may eventually try some RPF offenders, which would greatly elevate their legitimacy and reduce Hutu mistrust of the government. Gacacas are certainly more likely to do so than any other system of nationally-run courts, so on a comparative basis seem more likely to promote reconciliation than the alternatives.

International human rights groups and lawyers have mixed opinions about gacaca. Amnesty International writes that it "is concerned about a number of fundamental aspects of the proposals which do not conform to basic international standards for fair trial."[324] Human Rights Watch, on the other hand, takes a more positive view. In its 2002 *World Report,* it states, "Despite the absence of some basic guarantees of due process, the innovative system offered the only hope of trial within the foreseeable future for the tens of thousands now suffering inhumane conditions in prisons and communal lockups."[325]

The principal international concerns involve gacaca's lack of procedural guarantees, especially the prohibition against defense attorneys. In the eyes of international human rights activists, this is particularly troublesome given that state prosecutors and the 6th Chamber of the Supreme Court's legal advisors will be able to assist the gacaca.

Ironically, the government contends that this prohibition against defense attorneys is necessary for fairness. It claims that it cannot provide public attorneys, and that the vastly more rapid pace of the gacaca trials would overwhelm the international organizations that currently provide attorneys for suspects' defense. In this context, legal representation would effectively be available only to wealthy and powerful defendants.[326] The government did not want to establish a justice system that allowed the wealthy to "lawyer their way out" of accountability.

Fundamentally, these international concerns are predicated on a certain conception of fairness as procedure. Under this conception, stipulated procedural rights guarantee a fair trial. There is, however, an alternative view familiar to those of us raised in a common law-tradition. This is fairness through an empathetic trier of fact, commonly referred to as a "jury of one's peers." Particularly given Hutu suspicions of government-appointed judges and support of gacaca, it seems likely that they would by and large prefer fairness through an empathetic trier of fact. Under this conception of fairness, gacacas will be fairer than the government's genocide courts could ever be.

Gacaca's lack of procedural guarantees poses an additional problem. It appears to place gacaca justice in violation of two major human-rights covenants to which Rwanda is party: The *International Covenant on Civil and Political Rights* (ICCPR) and the *African (Banjul) Charter on Human Rights*. Article 14.3 of the ICCPR stipulates a number of judicial guarantees not provided by gacaca:[327]

> 14.3(b): To have adequate time and facilities for the preparation of his defense and to communicate with counsel of his own choosing
>
> 14.3(d): To be tried in his presence, and to defend himself in person or through legal assistance of his own choosing; to be informed, if he does not have legal assistance, of this right; and to have legal assistance assigned to him, in any case where the interests of justice so require, and without payment by him in any such case if he does not have sufficient means to pay for it.[328]

Article 7 of the *African Charter* contains similar language.[329]

The international donor community is largely supportive of gacaca, so the relevance of these violations is not immediately apparent.[330] However, the ICCPR requires that signatory states report violations observed in other signatory states. This could conceivably place international donors like the Belgian and American governments (which have given several million dollars to gacaca) in the awkward position of reporting to the ICCPR a violation that they have financially supported.[331]

Rwanda will need to seek derogation from its obligations under the ICCPR in order to avoid this potential conflict, which it is permitted to do in times of national emergency.[332] However, it is unclear how long a "national emergency" is permitted to last under the treaty; gacaca, after all, will take years. Rwanda is contemplating filing a formal notice with the UN and asking for a supportive vote on its position, which may eliminate potential problems.[333]

As a practical matter, Rwandan NGOs and the Rwandan government can promote fairness by carefully monitoring the gacaca process. Both have expressed their intention to do so. For example, LIPRODHOR, Rwanda's leading indigenous human-rights advocacy group, has had a project that monitored the fairness of the gacaca elections, and its field representatives will monitor the gacacas once they begin their work. They will be looking for evidence of witness intimidation, judicial bias, and the like. LIPRODHOR is pledged to publicizing any irregularities that it uncovers.[334] Ibuka, the survivors' organization, plans a similar program. This sort of spot-monitoring cannot alone guarantee that the gacacas' fairness. Some of the burden necessarily falls on suspects and victims to speak out and demand that judges exhibiting bias be replaced. The government also hopes that gacaca General Assemblies will monitor and regulate the actions of their Seats.[335]

One frequently neglected concern is the burden that gacaca will place on the judges. "Gacaca fatigue" is a serious concern. The judges will serve without compensation. Their terms are indefinite, and over a 5-plus year process their service will represent a major commitment of volunteer time and energy. They may resign at any time and be replaced by a vote of the General Assembly, but even so sustaining the judges' enthusiasm for service is crucial for the process to succeed.

On the other hand, gacaca may provide ancillary social benefits unrelated to its administration of justice. The October 2001 elections were the first of these. Rwanda has had dishearteningly little experience with free and fair elections. Even aside from the undemocratic tendencies of Rwandan governments, elections are often complicated by illiteracy—making balloting difficult—a tendency to increase ethnic tension, and severe shortages of paper and other voting necessities in the countryside. Against a history of electoral fraud, the gacaca elections have been widely hailed as free and fair.[336] The elections demonstrated to both the government and the Rwandan citizenry how a fair election could be held. The election's fairness may have also helped build confidence in the government's stated intent to democratize.

Finally, gacaca has the potential to help build Rwandan civil society and empower local communities to take greater responsibility over their affairs. The government sees this as a particular virtue as it tries to wean Rwandans from what was once a welfare state. Gacaca imbues local leaders with the idea that the community can play a significant role in its own governance, and will teach them the negotiating and compromise skills necessary for effective government.

Reasons for Hope

There are several reasons to be optimistic about the gacaca process. The first is the optimism of Rwandans themselves. An overwhelming majority support the process and express their intention to participate in it. Eighty to ninety percent of Rwandans participated in the elections.[337] Mention gacaca to even a poorly educated Rwandan, and he will give a well thought-out opinion that indicates that people are aware of the process and discussing it among themselves. After initial reluctance, even victims have come to accept gacaca, and Ibuka's support of the process will likely consolidate broader victim confidence in it. Given that gacaca is predicated on public involvement, this popular support is an auspicious beginning.

The success of the gacaca elections in 2001 is a further reason for hope. When the government first announced its plans for gacaca in 2000, few had any hope that elections could be held the following year.[338] The elections were delayed from their original early-summer date, but the government's proven ability to meet a timeline skeptics thought nearly impossible bodes well for gacaca's future.

Furthermore, gacaca has already begun to empower women within Rwandan society. Accounts of the elections indicate that women have played a much more significant role in gacaca than they have ever before played in any aspect of public life. Anecdotal evidence suggests that about a third of the elected gacaca judges are female.[339] Reporters have also been surprised by how forcefully women were willing to speak out during the elections and at the government's initial experiments with gacaca.[340] There is a general sense in Rwanda that women were the genocide's biggest losers. They lost their families, had their honor taken by rapists, and their property stolen. Many women's husbands are now in prison for their role in the genocide.[341] Women want to play a role in rebuilding a country others destroyed, and gacaca has afforded them the possibility of doing so. Once Rwandan women taste public life, one can hope that they will thirst for more.

Finally, one should be optimistic about gacaca because the only alternatives are dismal. Gacaca will not be perfect, but it is far superior to the present courts—whose pace effectively condemns genocide suspects to die in prison without the hope of a trial. These courts have done nothing to reduce ethnic tensions or promote healing in the countryside. A mass amnesty is equally unappealing, and would do little to either change Rwandan morality or reconcile badly divided Rwandans. Given the degree to which gacaca depends on public support—and considering these alternatives—we should be optimistic because gacaca is Rwanda's best hope.

5

CONCLUSION

No one doubts that gacaca is Rwanda's gamble. Failure, be it from judicial bias or witness reluctance, is an all too real possibility.

Gacaca is not yet set in stone, however. Problems may arise, but as they do steps can be taken to mitigate them. If witness security is a problem, perhaps more security agents in the countryside will be called for. If judicial incompetence is rife, trainers could offer remedial education to the judges. And so on. Rwanda can take a number of steps now, even before gacaca begins, in order to preempt such problems.

First, Rwanda needs to consider strategies to maintain judicial enthusiasm for the gacaca process.[342] This is particularly true of judges serving on higher-level gacacas, who will continue to hear cases long after the cell-level gacacas have finished their work. Compensation may be called for, or, if that is prohibitively expensive, establishing a term limit on judicial service and calling elections after several years. Those who wished to continue serving could seek re-election, while the rest would have a graceful opportunity to bow out.

Second, the Rwandan government must ensure that gacaca is adequately publicized. The current radio campaign and seminars should be continued, but the government should also initiate a concerted effort to bring elected local government officials into the informational campaign. Although Rwandans remain suspicious of the central government, preliminary evidence indicates a high degree of trust and respect for those officials they elected to local government councils.[343] These officials are therefore a logical target of any publicity campaign;

they can then be expected to spread the word and answer any questions that members of their communities pose.

Witness security measures are paramount. Witnesses will not testify if intimidated or so long as rumors of witness intimidation continue to circulate in the countryside.[344] A show of force may be helpful in this respect. The government does not have the resources necessary to guarantee the security of all witnesses, but it could temporarily dispatch security forces to regions where witnesses evince a particularly high level of fear.

Numerous witnesses will also need transportation from their current residence to the village they inhabited in 1994.[345] Given estimates that up to a million people have not returned to their pre-genocide residences, the government simply cannot afford to establish a witness transportation program based on individually transporting witnesses. It does intend to purchase as many vehicles as feasible to transport witnesses deemed particularly important; the rest will be left to their own devices.

Rwanda has an excellent intercity road system and well-developed network of minibuses that can ferry an individual from Kigali to almost any point in the country for under US $5, with many cities accessible for US $1–2. The vehicles involved are battered, overcrowded, and often run well behind schedule, but they do transport people to their destinations. The government could conceivably establish a voucher system whereby a witness's local gacaca or government office could give a witness a voucher valid for transit to the gacaca where the witness intends to testify. The destination gacaca could then provide a return ticket. The enterprising minibus drivers could redeem the vouchers at particular government offices throughout the country. Antifraud measures are needed, but can probably be developed. In theory, a government expenditure of a few hundred thousand dollars could provide for the transport of tens of thousands of witnesses. It is doubtful that all witnesses would be willing or able to participate in the program, but it could nonetheless dramatically expand the number of witnesses who testify.

NGOs must be encouraged to monitor the gacaca process to ensure its smooth functioning. Like human rights organizations everywhere, however, Rwandan NGOs are badly under-funded. The international grant making community should agree to financially support wide-spread monitoring efforts and could, if necessary, use its financial clout and international recognition to coerce the Rwandan government into acting to rectify any problems. Given Rwanda's low cost of labor, gacaca monitoring is a field in which a grant of a few hundred thousand dollars could have a tremendous impact on justice.

Finally, realistic expectations and flexibility are called for. The government, donors and the Rwandan people must all recognize that they are engaged in an experiment that will not be carried off perfectly—and that a flexible attitude and willingness to work correct problems will be essential to gacaca's success. Rwanda's officials clearly recognize this, and are prepared to make changes in gacaca as needed.[346] This bodes well for gacaca's long-term success.

Some Parting Thoughts:

The communitarian restorative model of transitional justice is not applicable everywhere. Rather, it is an approach meant to address the needs of a particular sort of transitional society: ones with a very high degree of complicity in human rights abuses, high rates of poverty, and intermixed settlement patterns that require victims and wrongdoers to return to the same communities.

Rwanda is precisely such a society, and gacaca—though developed as a cost-saving measure by a government unable to rebuild its regular courts and unwilling to let the genocide go unpunished—accords with the communitarian restorative ideal. If any form of justice can help Rwanda create a new moral ethic, lasting stability, and reconciliation, gacaca is it.

Rwanda is hardly the only country that could benefit from communitarian restorative justice. Sierra Leone, the Congo, Angola, Mozambique, the Sudan, Somalia: all these nations need reconciliation and moral education. The International Criminal Court, likely to be established later this year, will prosecute at most a few dozen top war criminals from each nation, out of the sight of the nations' peoples and doing little for reconciliation. That leaves tens to hundred of thousands of killers free to return home and take up residence alongside their victims without ever being condemned or even told that their actions were wrong. Communitarian restorative justice could be called upon to promote healing.

In some senses, Rwanda's ability to implement justice at all is an anomaly. The Rwandan government is able to talk of developing courts for the genocidaires only because the RPF won the civil war in 1994, and the defeated Habyarimana regime could not resist demands for justice. The communitarian restorative model of transitional justice cannot be implemented if a government lacks the will to put it in place—but then, no transitional justice could be.

If communitarian restorative justice can exist only in those rare situations where one side has won a civil war, what then is the point of discussing it? For one, the concept is helpful for thinking about Rwanda and its gacaca jurisdictions. International lawyers and other actors will be much more inclined to support gacaca if it is seen as an appropriate response to particular situation, rather than a sacrifice of justice on the alter of utility.

The communitarian restorative model is also useful *in case* other nations some day find themselves in Rwanda's situation. The existence of a model of transitional justice for such situations—particularly if gacaca proves the model's efficacy—will limit wrongdoers' ability to plead the impossibility of justice as a way of avoiding accountability. Rather than the close of a war evoking words of regret that poverty and backwardness preempt justice, a government can draw on the communitarian restorative model to begin healing its peoples' wounds.

In Rwanda, meanwhile, the training of judges commences on April 8th, 2002.[347] Eight years to the day after the genocide began in earnest, Rwanda is moving forward to finally close that tragic chapter in its national history.

BIBLIOGRAPHY:

Printed Sources:

Note: Page numbers designated with an asterisk (*) represent Lexis-Nexis' pagination system.

Agence France-Presse. "Three Suspects Go Before Rwanda Genocide Tribunal." 30 May 1996.

All Africa News Agency. "Plan Released for Shorter Trial Period in Rwanda." 11 May 1998.

Associated Press. "One Million Were Killed in Rwanda, Report Says." 15 February 2002.

Alvarez, Jose. "Crimes of States/Crimes of Hate: Lessons From Rwanda." *Yale Journal of International Law* 24 (Summer 1999).*365–*483.

Bass, Gary. *Stay the Hand of Vengeance.* Princeton: Princeton University Press, 2000.

Cassese, Antonio. "Reflections on International Criminal Justice." *Modern Law Review* 61 (January 1998). 1–10.

Cooper, David. "Hegel's Theory of Punishment," in Pelczynski, Z.A. (ed.). *Hegel's Political Philosophy: Problems and Perspectives.* Cambridge: Cambridge University Press, 1971. 151–167.

Crocker, David. "Truth Commissions, Transitional Justice, and Civil Society," in Rotberg, Robert, and Thompson, Dennis (eds.). *Truth v. Justice.* Princeton: Princeton University Press, 2000. 99–121.

Crossette, Barbara. "Experts Dispute Bush Aide's Criticism of War Crimes Panels." *The New York Times*. 2 March 2002. A1

Des Forges, Alison. *Leave None to Tell the Story*. New York: Human Rights Watch. 1999.

Dinner, Sinclair. "Restorative Justice and Civil Society in Melanesia: The Case of Papua New Guinea," in Srang, Heather, and Braithwaite, John (eds.). *Restorative Justice and Civil Society*. Cambridge: Cambridge University Press, 2001. 99–113.

Dowden, Richard. "No amnesty for Rwanda's Mass Killers." *The Independent:* 9 December 1994. 15.

Drumbl, Mark. "Punishment, Postgenocide. From Guilt to Shame to Civis in Rwanda." *New York University Law Review* 75 (November 2000).*1221–*1326.

Durkheim, Emile. "Crime and Punishment," in Lukes, Steven, and Scull, Andrew (eds.). *Durkheim and the Law*. New York: St. Martin's Press, 1983. 59–101.

Goldsmith, Charles. "Rwandan Capital Calm, French Troops Arrive." *United Press International:* 5 October 2000.

Goldstone, Richard. *For Humanity: Reflections of a War Crimes Investigator*. New Haven: Yale University Press, 2000.

Gourevitch, Philip. *We Wish to Inform You That Tomorrow We Will Be Killed With Our Families: Stories from Rwanda*. New York: Farrar, Strauss, and Giroux, 1998.

Greenway, H.D.S. "Voices of Conflict in the Mideast." *Boston Globe:* 15 March 2002. A19.

Gutman, Amy, and Thompson, Dennis, "The Moral Foundations of Truth Commissions," in Rotberg, Robert, and Thompson, Dennis (eds.). *Truth v. Justice.* Princeton: Princeton University Press, 2000. 22–44.

Hampton, Jean, "Moral Education Theory of Punishment." *Philosophy and Public Affairs* 13,3 (Summer 1984). 208–238.

Hirondelle News Agency, "Women Take Center Stage in Election of 'People's Judges.'" 4 October 2001.

Huntington, Samuel. *The Third Wave.* Norman: University of Oklahoma Press, 1991.

Huyse, Luc. "Justice After Transitions: On the Choices Successor Elites Make in Dealing with the Past," in Kritz, Neil (ed.). *Transitional Justice Volume 1: General Considerations.* Washington: US Institute of Peace Press, 1995. 104–115.

Internews. "Gacaca: Genocide Suspects Look Forward to New Justice System." 6 October 2001.

Kakwenzire, Joan, and Kamukama, Dixon. "The Development and Consolidation of Extremist Forces in Rwanda: 1990–1994," in Adelman, Howard, and Suhrke, Astri (eds.). *The Path of a Genocide.* New Brunswick: Transaction Publishers, 2000.

Kiss, Elizabeth. "Moral Ambition Within and Beyond Political Constraints; Reflections on Restorative Justice," in Rotberg, Robert, and Thompson, Dennis (eds.). *Truth v. Justice.* Princeton: Princeton University Press, 2000. 68–98.

Lemarchand, Réne. *Rwanda and Burundi.* New York: Praeger, 1970.

Minnow, Martha. *Between Vengeance and Forgiveness: Facing History after Genocide and Mass Violence.* Boston: Beacon Press, 1998.

Minnow, Martha. "Hope for Healing: What Can Truth Commissions Do?" in Rotberg, Robert, and Thompson, Dennis (eds.). *Truth v. Justice.* Princeton: Princeton University Press, 2000. 235–260.

Maier, "Doing History, Doing Justice: The Narrative of the Historian and of the Truth Commission," in Rotberg, Robert, and Thompson, Dennis (eds.). *Truth v. Justice.* Princeton: Princeton University Press, 2000. 261–278.

Mamdani, Mahmood. *When Victims Become Killers.* Kampala: Fountain Publishers, 2001.

Maykuth, A. "Rwanda Swamped by Refugee Flood." *Courier-Mail:* 18 November 1996.

McGreal, Chris. "Rwanda Genocide Trials Get off the Ground." *Mail and Guardian:* 31 May 1996.

Morris, Madeline H. "Justice in the Wake of Genocide: Rwanda," in Cooper, Belinda (ed.), *War Crimes: The Legacy of Nuremburg.* New York: TV Books, 1999. 210–228.

Mucyo, Jean De Dieu. "Gacaca Courts and Genocide." In Villa-Vicencio, Charles and Savage, Tyrone (eds.). *Rwanda and South Africa in Dialogue.* Cape Town: Institute for Justice and Reconciliation, 2001.

Neuffer, Elizabeth. *The Key To my Neighbors House: Seeking Justice in Bosnia and Rwanda.* New York: Picador, 2001.

Newbury, Catherine. *The Cohesion of Oppression.* New York: Columbia University Press, 1988.

Nino, Carlos Santiago. *Radical Evil on Trial.* New Haven: Yale University Press, 1996.

Nozick, Robert. *Philosophical Explanations.* Cambridge MA: Belknap Press, 1981.

Orentlicher, Diane. "Settling Accounts: The Duty to Prosecute Human Rights Violations of a Prior Regime," in Kritz, Neil (ed.). *Transitional Justice Volume 1: General Considerations.* Washington: US Institute of Peace Press, 1995. 475–416.

Osiel, Mark. *Mass Atrocity, Collective Memory, and the Law.* New Brunswick: Transaction Publishers, 1997.

Press, Robert. "Rwandan Leader Says 100,000 Should be Tried for War Crimes." *Christian Science Monitor:* 9 August 1994.

Prunier, Gérard. *The Rwanda Crisis.* Kampala: Fountain Publishers, 1995.

Randal, Jonathan. "1st Genocide Trial is Near in Rwanda." *Chicago Sun-Times:* 5 March 1995. 32.

Republic of Rwanda, "Organic Law 40/2000 of 26/01/2001 Setting Up Gacaca Jurisdictions and Organizing Prosecutions for Offenses Constituting the Crime of Genocide or Crimes Against Humanity Committed Between October 1, 1999 and December 31st, 1994." *Official Gazette of the Republic of Rwanda* (October 2000). 33–65. Referenced as "Gacaca Law."

Schmidt, William. "Refugee Missionaries from Rwanda Speak their Terror, Grief and Guilt." *New York Times:* 12 April 1994: A6

Speake, John Hanning. *Journal of the Discovery of the Source of the Nile.* Mineola: Dover Publications, 1996.

Stillman, Peter. "Hegel's Idea of Punishment." *Journal of the History of Philosophy* 24, v. 2 (April 1976). 169–182.

Teitel, Ruti. "Transitional Jurisprudence: The Role of Law in Political Transformation." *Yale Law Journal* 106 (May, 1997).*2009–*2080.

Tunbridge, Louise. "Rwanda Trial Marks Grim Anniversary." *Daily Telegraph:* 7 Aprile 1995. 14.

United Nations Integrated Regional Information Network, "Rwanda: Democratisation Process Underway—Kagame." 11 April 2001.

University of Rwanda Center for Conflict Management, Les Jurisdictions Gacaca et le Processus de Réconciliation Nationale. Butare: National University of Rwanda, 2000.

Young, Crawford. *The Politics of Cultural Pluralism.* Madison: University of Wisconsin Press, 1976.

Electronic Sources:

Amnesty International. "Rwanda: The Troubled Course of Justice." 26 April 2000.
**<http://web.amnesty.org/802568F7005C4453/0/
00B458F4B18051F2802568BF004A5937?Open>**

Amnesty USA. "International Criminal Court." 4 April 2002.
<http://www.amnesty-usa.org/icc/>

Braithwaite, John. "Restorative Justice and a Better Future." *RealJustice.* 26 October 1996.
<http://www.realjustice.org/Pages/braithwaite.html>

Coalition for the International Criminal Court. "Timeline."
<http://www.igc.org/icc/html/timeline.htm>

Drumtra, Jeff. "Rwanda Refugee Report, Part 2." *U.S. Committee for Refugees:* 25 October 1995.
<http://www.africaaction.org/docs95/rwan9511.2.htm>

Embassy of Rwanda in Washington, D.C. "The Judicial System in Rwanda: A Report on Justice."
<http://www.rwandemb.org/justice/justice.htm>

Hirondelle News Agency. "Training of Gacaca Judges Starts April 8th, 2002." 3 April 2002.
<http://www.hirondelle.org/hirondelle.nsf/ caefd9edd48f5826c12564cf004f793d/ e50bea4b77a0482bc1256763005ac92a?OpenDocument>

Human Rights Watch. "World Report 1997: Rwanda." 1997.
<http://www.hrw.ord/worldreport/Africa-10.htm#P816_217123>

Human Rights Watch. "World Report 2001: Rwanda." 2001.
<http://www.hrw.org/wr2k1/africa/rwanda.html>

Human Rights Watch. "World Report 2002: Rwanda." 2002.
<http://www.hrw.org.wr2k2/africa9.html>

Integrated Regional Information Network. "Central And Eastern Africa: Update 340." 26 January 1998.
<http://www.sas.upenn.edu/African_Studies/Hornet/ irin340.html>

International Criminal Tribunal for Rwanda. "General Information."
<http://www.ictr.org>

International Criminal Tribunal for Rwanda. "Judgment and Sentence of Clement Kayishema (ICTR-95-01)." 21 May 1999.
<http://www.ictr.org>

Johns Hopkins University Center for Communication Programs and *Rwandan Ministry of Justice.* "Perceptions About the Gacaca Law in Rwanda." April 2001.
<http://www.jhuccp.org/centerpubs/sp_19/English/>

Kaberuka, Donald. "2002 Budget Statement." *Republic of Rwanda Ministry of Finance and Economic Planning.* 26 November 2001.
<http://www.minecofin.gov.rw/ministry/minister/speeches/ 2001_11_26_budget_year_2002.htm>

Kumar, Krishna. "The International Response to Conflict and Genocide: Lessons from the Rwanda Experience." *Journal of Humanitarian Assistance.*
<http://www.reliefweb.int/library/nordic/book4/pb024e.html>

Paul McCold. "Police-Facilitated Restorative Conferencing: What the Data Show." *RealJustice.* November 1998.
<http://www.fp.enter.net/restorativepractices/policeconferencing.pdf.>

McCold, Paul. "Restorative Justice: The Role of the Community." *RealJustice.* March 1995.
<http://www.realjustice.org/Pages/community3.html>

Remember Chile. "Introduction: Pinochet's Arrest." 29 November 2001.
<http://www.remember-chile.org.uk/beginners/index.htm>

Rauch, Jonathan. "Seeing Around Corners." *The Atlantic Online.* April 2002.
<http://www.theatlantic.com/issues/2002/04/rauch.htm>

UNICEF. "Rwanda." 1 February 2002.
<http://www.unicef.org/statis/Country_1Page145.html>

The World Bank. "GNI Per Capita 2000." 2000.
<http://www.worldbank.org/data/databytopic/GNPPC.pdf>

The World Bank. "Rwanda at a Glance." 17 September 2001.
<http://www.worldbank.org/data/countrydata/aag/rwa_aag.pdf>

Treaties and Laws:

African (Banjul) Charter of Human Rights. Adopted 27 June 1981, entered into force 21 October 1986.
<http://www1.umn.edu/humanrts/instree/z1afchar.htm>

International Covenant on Civil and Political Rights (ICCPR). Ratified 16 December 1966, entered into force 23 March 1976. **<http://www.unhchr.ch/html/menu3/b/a_ccpr.htm>**

Republic of Rwanda, "Organic Law 40/2000 of 26/01/2001 Setting Up Gacaca Jurisdictions and Organizing Prosecutions for Offenses Constituting the Crime of Genocide or Crimes Against Humanity Committed Between October 1, 1999 and December 31st, 1994." *Official Gazette of the Republic of Rwanda* (October 2000). 33–65. Referenced as "Gacaca Law."

Interviews:

Klaas De Jonge, Penal Reform International. Interview by Author. Kigali, Rwanda: 12 January 2002. Tape on File with author.

Erwin De Wandal, Belgian Mission to Rwanda. Interview by Author. Kigali, Rwanda: 18 January 2002. Tape on file with author.

Gerard Gahima, Prosecutor General. Interview by Author. Kigali, Rwanda: 9 January 2002. Tape on File with author.

M. Goretti, Trocaire. Interview by Author. Kigali, Rwanda: 10 January 2002. Tape on File with author.

Aloys Habimana, LIPRODHOR. Interview by Author. Kigali, Rwanda: 15 January 2002. Tape on File with author.

Isabelle Kalihangabo, 6th Chamber of the Rwandan Supreme Court. Interview by Author. Kigali, Rwanda: 18 January 2002. Tape on file with author.

Jean Karambizi, Johns Hopkins University Center for Communications Programs. Interview by Author. Kigali, Rwanda: 10 January 2002. Tape on File with author.

Kassim Kayira, Internews. Interview by Author. Kigali, Rwanda: 9 January 2002. Tape on File with author.

Antoine Mugasera, Ibuka. Interview by Author. Kigali, Rwanda: 11 January 2002. Tape on File with author.

Kimberly Pease, USAID Kigali. Interview by Author. Kigali, Rwanda: 10 January 2002. Tape on file with author.

St. Hilaire, Pierre, USAID Kigali. Interview by Author. Kigali, Rwanda: 18 January 2002. Tape on File with author.

Van Cutsem, Chantal, Lawyers Without Borders. Interview by Author. Kigali, Rwanda: 15 January 2002. Tape on File with author.

PLEDGE PAGE

This paper represents my own work in accordance with University regulations.

Endnotes

[1]. ICTR Judgment of Clément Kayishema. Sections 5.2–5.3.

[2]. Ibid. Section 5.3, line 329.

[3]. Ibid. Section 5.3, lines 331-332.

[4]. Ibid. Section 5.3, line 332.

[5]. Chris McGreal, "Rwanda Genocide Trials Get off the Ground."

[6]. Agence France-Presse, "Three suspects go before Rwanda genocide tribunal."

[7]. ICTR, "Judgement of Clément Kayishema" Article 8.

[8]. Alvarez, "Crimes of States/Crimes of Hate." 2.

[9]. Ibid., 5.

[10]. *Remember Chile,* "Introduction: Pinochet's Arrest."

[11]. Drumbl, "Punishment, Postgenocide: From Guilt to Shame To Civis in Rwanda." 2.

[12]. Des Forges, *Leave None to Tell the Story.* 753.

[13]. Interview with Klaas De Jonge.

[14]. Mahmood Mamdani, *When Victims Become Killers.* Back Cover.

[15]. WorldBank, "Rwanda at a Glance."

[16]. All Africa News Agency, "Plan Released for Shorter Trial Period in Rwanda."

[17]. William Schmidt, "Refugee Missionaries From Rwanda Speak of Their Terror, Grief and Guilt."

[18].   Cited in Lemarchand, *Rwanda and Burundi*. 48.

[19].   Prunier, *The Rwanda Crisis*. 5

[20].   Ibid. 9.

[21].   Ibid. 11.

[22].   Ibid. 12.

[23].   Mamdani, *When Victims Become Killers,* 45.

[24].   Ibid. 46.

[25].   Ibid. 10.

[26].   Newbury, *The Cohesion of Oppression*. 11.

[27].   Cited in Ibid.12.

[28].   Ibid. 40.

[29].   Ibid. 40.

[30].   Mamdani, *When Victims Become Killers*. 69.

[31].   Newbury, *The Cohesion of Oppression*. 51.

[32].   Mamdani, *When Victims Become Killers*. 63.

[33].   Newbury, *The Cohesion of Oppression*. 79-81

[34].   Ibid. 98-99.

[35].   Ibid. Chapter 7.

[36].   Mamdani, *When Victims Become Killers*. 70.

[37].   John Hanning Speke, *Journal of the Discovery of the Source of the Nile*. 241.

[38].   Mamdani, *When Victims Become Killers*. 82.

[39].   Ibid 86.

[40].   Cited in Prunier, *The Rwanda Crisis*. 6

[41].   Cited in Ibid. 6

[42]. Lemarchand, *Rwanda and Burundi.* 66.

[43]. Ibid. 72.

[44]. Prunier, *The Rwanda Crisis.* 27.

[45]. Ibid. 27.

[46]. Newbury, *Cohesion of Oppression.* 140.

[47]. Ibid. 112.

[48]. Prinier, *The Rwanda Crisis.* 27.

[49]. Ibid. 33.

[50]. Ibid. 14.

[51]. Mamdani, *When Victims Become Killers.* 98-99.

[52]. Des Forges, *Leave None to Tell the Story.* 38.

[53]. Prunier, *The Rwanda Crisis.* 43.

[54]. Jean-Jacques Maquet and Marcel d'Hertefelt, cited in Prunier, *The Rwanda Crisis.* 43.

[55]. Mamdani, *When Victims Become Killers.* 115.

[56]. Ibid. 116.

[57]. Ibid. 116.

[58]. Ibid. 116.

[59]. Ibid. 116.

[60]. Ibid. 116.

[61]. Cited in, Ibid. 116.

[62]. Lemarchand, *Rwanda and Burundi.* 150.

[63]. Mamdani, *When Victims Become Killers.* 47.

[64]. Prunier, *The Rwanda Crisis.* 48.

[65]. Lemarchand, *Rwanda and Burundi.* 154.

[66]. Ibid. 155.

[67]. Young, *The Politics of Cultural Pluralism.* 156.

[68]. Lemarchand, *Rwanda and Burundi.* 156.

[69]. Ibid. 157-158.

[70]. Cited in Lemarchand, *Rwanda and Burundi.*159.

[71]. Prunier, *The Rwanda Crisis.* 49.

[72]. Cited in Ibid. 51.

[73]. Lemarchand, *Rwanda and Burundi.* 173.

[74]. Ibid.181.

[75]. Cited in Ibid.183.

[76]. Ibid.193.

[77]. Prunier, *The Rwanda Crisis.* 57.

[78]. Ibid. 59.

[79]. Des Forges, *Leave None to Tell the Story.* 40.

[80]. Cited in Lemarchand, *Rwanda and Burundi.*169.

[81]. Prunier, *The Rwanda Crisis.* 75.

[82]. Ibid. 75.

[83]. Cited in Ibid. 76.

[84]. Ibid. 78.

[85]. Ibid. 78.

[86]. Ibid. 81.

[87]. Ibid. 81.

[88]. Ibid. 84.

[89]. Des Forges, *Leave None to Tell the Story.* 46.

[90]. Ibid. 47.

[91]. Ibid. 47.

[92]. Prunier, *The Rwanda Crisis.* 64.

[93]. Ibid. 66.

[94]. Ibid. 67.

[95]. Ibid. 70.

[96]. Ibid. 72.

[97]. Mamdani, *When Victims Become Killers.* 175.

[98]. Ibid. 173.

[99]. Ibid. 175.

[100]. Ibid. 182.

[101]. Ibid. 176.

[102]. Ibid. 177-178.

[103]. Ibid. 179.

[104]. Ibid. 181.

[105]. Ibid. 183.

[106]. Ibid. 186.

[107]. Ibid. 186.

[108]. Ibid. 186.

[109]. Ibid. 186.

[110]. Des Forges, *Leave None to Tell the Story.* 50

[111]. Charles Goldsmith, "Rwandan Capital Calm, French Troops Arrive."

[112]. This is a theme that runs throughout Professor Prunier's *The Rwanda Crisis.*

[113]. Des Forges, *Leave None to Tell the Story.* 77.

[114]. Ibid. 78.

[115]. Cited in Des Forges, *Leave None to Tell the Story.* 50

[116]. Des Forges, *Leave None to Tell the Story.*

[117]. Joan Kakwenzire and Dixon Kamukama, "The Development and Consolidation of Extremist Forces in Rwanda 1990-1994." 69.

[118]. Ibid. 70.

[119]. Ibid.

[120]. Des Forges, *Leave None to Tell the Story.* 89.

[121]. Prunier, *The Rwanda Crisis.* 146.

[122]. Ibid. 166.

[123]. Ibid. 169.

[124]. Des Forges, *Leave None to Tell the Story.* 75.

[125]. Prunier, *The Rwanda Crisis.* 168.

[126]. Des Forges, *Leave None to Tell the Story.* 125.

[127]. Ibid. 122.

[128]. Ibid. 124.

[129]. Ibid. 134.

[130]. Ibid. 137-138.

[131]. Ibid. 141.

[132]. Prunier, *The Rwanda Crisis.* 211.

[133]. Des Forges, *Leave None to Tell the Story.*181-186.

[134]. Prunier, *The Rwanda Crisis.* 222.

[135]. Ibid. 236.

[136]. Ibid. 243.

[137]. Des Forges, *Leave None to Tell the Story.* 202.

[138]. Ibid. 440-446.

[139]. Prunier, *The Rwanda Crisis.* 270.

[140]. Cited in Des Forges, *Leave None to Tell The Story.* 251.

[141]. Annette Seegers, African Politics 364 at Princeton University.

[142]. Cited in Prunier, *The Rwanda Crisis.* 247.

[143]. Des Forges, *Leave None to Tell the Story.* 262

[144]. Cited in Ibid. 261.

[145]. Interview with Scott Strauss.

[146]. Ibid. 294

[147]. Ibid. 263.

[148]. Ibid. 265.

[149]. Associated Press, "One million were killed in Rwanda, report says."

[150]. Interview with Scott Strauss.

[151]. Initial figures are from Prunier, *The Rwanda Crisis.* 365. Current figure is drawn from an interview with Klaas De Jonge.

[152]. Interview with Klass De Jonge.

[153]. Krishna Kumar, "The International Response to Conflict and Genocide: Lessons from the Rwanda Experience—Chapter 1."

[154]. U.S. Committee for Refugees, "Rwanda Refugee Report, Part 2."

[155]. See, for example, A. Maykuth, "Rwanda Swamped By Refugee Flood."

[156]. UN Integrated Regional Information Network, "Rwanda: Democratisation Process Underway—Kagame."

[157]. Human Rights Watch, "World Report 2001: Rwanda."

[158]. Worldbank, "GNI Per Capita 2000."

[159]. UNICEF, "Statistics."

[160]. The title is borrowed from Carlos Nino's work, *Radical Evil on Trial*

[161]. Richard Dowden, "No amnesty for Rwanda's Mass Killers."

[162]. Jean De Dieu Mucyo, "Gacaca Courts and Genocide." 49.

[163]. Rwanda Embassy, "The Judicial System in Rwanda." Table 1.

[164]. Des Forges, *Leave None to Tell the Story.* 748

[165]. Robert Press, "Rwandan Leader Says 100,000 Should be Tried for War Crimes."

[166]. Jonathan Randal, "1st Genocide Trial is Near in Rwanda."

[167]. Louise Tunbridge, "Rwanda Trial Marks Grim Anniversary."

[168]. Human Rights Watch, "1997 World Report, Rwanda."

[169]. Amnesty International, "The Troubled Course of Justice."

[170]. Madeline Morris, "Justice in the Wake Of Genocide." 221.

[171]. Carlos Nino, *Radical Evil on Trial.*20-26.

[172]. Carlos Nino, *Radical Evil on Trial.* 33-36.

[173]. Coalition for the ICC, "Timeline."

[174]. Coalition for the ICC, "Timeline."

[175]. Amnesty International, "Countdown to the International Criminal Court."

[176]. Antonio Cassese, "Reflections on International Criminal Justice." 6-8.

[177]. Ibid." 4-5.

[178]. David Crocker, "Truth Commissions, Transitional Justice, and Civil Society." 105.

[179]. Jose Alvarez, "Crimes of States/Crimes of Hate." 2.

[180]. Samuel Huntington, *The Third Wave. 213.*

[181]. Ibid. 213.

[182]. Antonio Cassese, "Reflections on International Criminal Justice." 2.

[183]. Ibid. 6.

[184]. Ibid. 3.

[185]. Ibid. 6.

[186]. Ibid. 6.

[187]. Luc Huyse, "Justice after Transition." 340.

[188]. Cited in, Ibid, "Justice after Transition." 341.

[189]. Ruti Teitel, "Transitional Jurisprudence." 6.

[190]. Ibid. 6.

[191]. Diane Orentlicher, 377.

[192]. See, for example, Diane Orentlicher, "Settling Accounts." 377.

[193]. Ibid. 377.

[194]. Jean De Dieu Mucyo, "Gacaca Courts and Genocide." 49.

[195]. Cassese, "Reflections on International Criminal Justice." 3.

[196]. Ibid. 3.

[197]. Cassese, "Reflections on International Criminal Justice." 6.

[198]. Gary Bass, *Stay the Hand of Vengeance.* 291.

[199]. Jonathan Rauch, "Seeing Around Corners."

[200]. H.D.S. GREENWAY, "Voices of Conflict in the Mideast." A19.

[201]. For a very interesting, in depth analysis of these events, see Carlos Nino, *Radical Evil on Trial.* Chapter 2, 41-104.

[202]. South Africa's TRC, for example, was a compromise made in large part to speed the end of apartheid.

[203]. See, for example, Charles S. Maier, "Doing History, Doing Justice."

[204]. Peter Stillman, "Hegel's Idea of Punishment." 169.

[205]. Ibid. 170.

[206]. Ibid.170.

[207]. Ibid.171.

[208]. Ibid. 171.

[209]. Ibid. 171.

[210]. David Cooper, "Hegel's Theory of Punishment." 162.

[211]. See, for example, Carlos Nino, *Radical Evil on Trial.* 143-148.

[212]. Carlos Nino, *Radical Evil on Trial.* 148.

[213]. Cassese, "Reflections on International Criminal Justice." 1.

[214]. Amy Gutmann and Dennis Thompson, "The Moral Foundations of Truth Commissions." 31.

[215]. See Mark Osiel, *Mass Atrocity, Collective Memory, and the Law.* 64-72.

[216]. Jean De Dieu Mucyo, "Gacaca Courts and Genocide."

[217]. All Africa News Agency, "Plan Released for Shorter Trial Period in Rwanda."

[218]. Interview with Klass De Jonge.

[219]. Amnesty International, "The Troubled Course of Justice."

[220]. Ibid.

[221]. Donald Kaberuka, "2002 Budget Statement."

[222]. ICTR, "General Information."

[223]. Human Rights Watch, "World Report 2001: Rwanda."

[224]. Jose Alvarez, "Crimes of States/Crimes of Hate." 3.

[225]. Emile Durkheim, "Crime and Punishment." 69.

[226]. Ibid. 69.

[227]. Ibid. 69.

[228]. Drumbl, "Punishment, Postgenocide: From Guilt to Shame to Civis in Rwanda." 12.

[229]. Ibid. 27.

[230]. Gourevitch, *We Wish to Inform You.* 123.

[231]. Jean Hampton, Moral Education Theory of Punishment. 212.

[232]. Ibid. 212.

[233]. H.P. Grice, "Meaning." The Philosophical Review. 384.

[234]. Nozick, *Philosophical Explanations.* 374.

[235]. Ibid. 384.

[236]. Ibid. 379.

[237]. Jean Hampton, "Moral Education Theory of Punishment." 216.

[238]. Ibid. 218.

[239]. Ibid. 220.

[240]. Drumbl, "Punishment, Postgenocide: From Guilt to Shame to Civis in Rwanda." 4.

[241]. Ibid. 4.

[242]. Drumbl, "Punishment, Postgenocide: From Guilt to Shame to Civis in Rwanda." 4.

[243]. Alvarez, "Crimes of States/Crimes of Hate." 23.

[244]. Ibid. 23.

[245]. Interview with Klaas De Jonge.

[246]. Braithwaite, "Restorative Justice and a Better Future." 3.

[247]. Drumbl, "Punishment, Postgenocide: From Guilt to Shame to Civis in Rwanda." 14.

[248]. Ibid. 14.

[249]. Braithwaite, "Restorative Justice and a Better Future." 3.

[250]. Ibid. 4.

[251]. Ibid. 4.

[252]. Paul McCold, "Restorative Justice: The Role of the Community." 3.

[253]. Braithwaite, "Restorative Justice and a Better Future." 4.

[254]. See, for example, Paul McCold, "Police-Facilitated Restorative Conferencing: What the Data Show."

[255]. Braithwaite and Strang, *Restorative Justice and Civil Society.* 5.

[256]. Sinclair Dinner, "Restorative Justice and Civil Society in Melanesia." 99-113.

[257]. John Braithwaite, *Crime, Shame and Reintegration.*12-13.

[258]. Ibid. 12-13.

[259]. Drumbl, "Punishment, Postgenocide: From Guilt to Shame to Civis in Rwanda." 14.

[260]. John Braithwaite, *Crime, Shame and Reintegration.* 55.

[261]. Drumbl, "Punishment, Postgenocide: From Guilt to Shame to Civis in Rwanda." 15.

[262]. John Braithwaite, *Crime, Shame and Reintegration.* 55.

[263]. Drumbl, "Punishment, Postgenocide: From Guilt to Shame to Civis in Rwanda." 15.

[264]. Braithwaite, "Restorative Justice and a Better Future."

[265]. Interview with Klass De Jonge.

[266]. Interview with Gerard Gahima

[267]. Gacaca Law, Preamble.

[268]. National University of Rwanda, *Les Jurisdictions Gacaca et les Processus de Réconciliation Nationale.* 31.

[269]. Ibid. 32.

[270]. Ibid. 32.

[271]. Ibid. 32.

[272]. Jennifer Widner, "Courts and Democracy in Postconflict Transitions."*66.

[273]. National University of Rwanda, *Les Jurisdictions Gacaca et les Processus de Réconciliation Nationale.* 34. Also, interview with M. Goretti.

[274]. Ibid. 34.

[275]. Interview with Gerard Gahima.

[276]. These categories were originally defined in Organic Law No 08/96 of August 30, 1996. Articles 2 and 3.

[277]. Rwandan Supreme Court and Lawyers Without Borders, *Manuel Explicatif.* 17

[278]. Interview with Klaas De Jonge.

[279]. Interview with Chantal van Cutsem

[280]. Gacaca Law, Articles 1, 3, 4.

[281]. Ibid, Articles 5-9.

[282]. Rwandan Supreme Court and Lawyers Without Borders, *Manuel Explicatif.* Chapter 4. 38-48.

[283]. Interview with Chantal van Cutsem.

[284]. Rwandan Supreme Court and Lawyers Without Borders, *Manuel Explicatif.* Chapter 7. 103-153.

[285]. Ibid. Chapter 7, Part 7. 147-153.

[286]. Interview with Isabelle Kalihangabo.

[287]. Interview with Klaas De Jonge.

[288]. Interview with Chantal van Cutsem.

[289]. Rwandan Supreme Court and Lawyers Without Borders, *Manuel Explicatif.* Chapter 7, Part 4. 129-132.

[290]. Johns Hopkins University, *Perceptions.* 15.

[291]. Interview with Aloys Habimana.

[292]. Interview with Kassim Kayira.

[293]. Interview with Klaas de Jonge.

[294]. Gacaca Law, Article 10.

[295]. Ibid, Article 11.

[296]. Interview with Kassim Kayira.

[297]. Interview with Aloys Habimana.

[298]. Interview with Chantal van Cutsem.

[299]. Ibid.

[300]. Ibid.

[301]. *Hirondelle News Agency,* "Training of Gacaca Judges Starts April 8th, 2002."

[302]. Interview with Aloys Habimana.

[303]. *Integrated Regional Information Network,* "Central And Eastern Africa: Update 340."

[304]. Johns Hopkins University, *Perceptions.* 14.

[305]. Interview with Jean Karambizi.

[306]. Ibid.

[307]. Interview with Antoine Mugasera.

[308]. Johns Hopkins University, *Perceptions*. Also, multiple interviews.

[309]. Interview with Beatrice Murebwayire.

[310]. Ibid.

[311]. Johns Hopkins University, *Perceptions*.

[312]. *Internews,* "Genocide Suspects Look Forward to New Justice
System."

[313]. Barbara Crossette, "Experts Dispute Bush Aide's Criticism of
War Crimes Panels."

[314]. Gacaca Law, Article 12.

[315]. Interview with Chantal van Cutsem.

[316]. Interview with Kassim Kayira.

[317]. Ibid.

[318]. Ibid.

[319]. Rwandan Supreme Court and Lawyers Without Borders, *Manuel Explicatif.* 40.

[320]. Interview with Jean Karambizi.

[321]. Interview with Beatrice Murebwayire.

[322]. Interview with Antoine Mugasera.

[323]. Conversation with Scott Strauss, a former Nairobi-based journalist.

[324]. Amnesty International, *The Troubled Course of Justice.*

[325]. Human Rights Watch, "2002 World Report."

[326]. Interview with Gerard Gahima.

[327]. ICCPR, Article 4.

[328]. Ibid.

[329]. *Banjul Charter.*

[330]. Interview with Erwin De Wandel.

[331]. Ibid.

[332]. Ibid.

[333]. Ibid.

[334]. Interview with Aloys Habimana.

[335]. Interview with Gerard Gahima.

[336]. Interviews with Kassim Kayira and Aloys Habimana.

[337]. Interview with Klaas De Jonge.

[338]. Interview with Chantal van Cutsem.

[339]. Hirondelle News Agency, "Women Take Center Stage in Election of 'People's Judges."

[340]. Ibid."

[341]. Interview with Kassim Kayira.

[342]. Interview with Chantal van Cutsem.

[343]. Interview with Klaas De Jonge.

[344]. Interview with Kassim Kayira.

[345]. Ibid.

[346]. Interview with Gerard Gahima.

[347]. *Hirondelle News Agency,* "Training of Gacaca Judges Starts April 8th, 2002."

0-595-27052-2

Made in the USA
Monee, IL
05 December 2020